THEOLOGY OF LOVE IN THE TEACHINGS OF APOSTLE PAUL

Dr. Maxwell Shimba

Printed in the United States of America

SHIMBA
PUBLISHING

TABLE OF CONTENTS

INTRODUCTION

Apostle Paul, one of the most influential figures in early Christianity, provides a profound and comprehensive theology of love throughout his epistles. His teachings on love are not merely theoretical but are grounded in practical applications for individuals and communities. This book aims to explore the theology of love as presented by Apostle Paul, drawing insights from his letters and their implications for contemporary Christian living.

Paul's writings are marked by an unwavering emphasis on love as the core of Christian faith and practice. His understanding of love is deeply rooted in the person and work of Jesus Christ, whom he describes as the ultimate manifestation of God's love for humanity. For Paul, love is not an abstract concept but a dynamic force that transforms lives, reconciles relationships, and builds up the body of Christ.

In a world that often seems devoid of genuine love and compassion, Paul's teachings offer a timeless and transformative message. His letters address diverse contexts and challenges faced by the early Christian communities, yet his central theme of love remains constant. Whether admonishing the Corinthians for their divisions, encouraging the Galatians in their newfound freedom, or exhorting the Ephesians to unity and maturity, Paul consistently points to love as the essential ingredient for authentic Christian living.

This book is structured to provide a detailed exploration of Paul's theology of love as it unfolds in his various epistles. We will delve into his foundational teachings on love in 1 Corinthians 13, examine the relationship between love and the law in Romans, and consider how love functions within the Christian community as described in Ephesians. Additionally, we will explore Paul's insights on the sacrificial nature of love in Philippians, the sustaining power of love in times of suffering in 2 Corinthians, and the interplay between love and holiness in 1 Thessalonians.

As we journey through Paul's letters, we will see how his theology of love is not only doctrinally rich but also immensely practical. Paul calls believers to embody love in their everyday lives, urging them to serve one another selflessly, to bear with one another patiently, and to build each other up in faith. His vision of love is holistic, encompassing every aspect of the Christian experience—from personal devotion to communal worship, from ethical behavior to spiritual maturity.

In an age where the true meaning of love is often misunderstood or diluted, Paul's teachings offer clarity and depth. They challenge us to go beyond superficial expressions of affection and to embrace a love that is sacrificial, enduring, and transformative. This love, as Paul articulates, is the very essence of the gospel and the mark of genuine discipleship.

As you read through this book, I invite you to engage with Paul's writings afresh and to allow his profound insights on love to inspire and guide you. May his teachings lead you to a deeper understanding of the love of God and a greater commitment to living out that love in every sphere of life.

Dr. Maxwell Shimba

DR. MAXWELL SHIMBA

CHAPTER 01

THE FOUNDATION OF LOVE

1 Corinthians 13: The Greatest of These is Love

The Context of 1 Corinthians 13: Understanding the Corinthian Church and the Issues Paul Addresses

1 Corinthians 13 is often referred to as the "Love Chapter" and is one of the most well-known and frequently quoted passages in the New Testament. To fully appreciate the depth and significance of Paul's message in this chapter, it is essential to understand the context in which it was written. The church in Corinth was a vibrant but troubled community, facing numerous challenges and conflicts that threatened their unity and spiritual growth.

The Corinthian Church

The city of Corinth was a bustling metropolis known for its economic prosperity, cultural diversity, and moral laxity. As a major port city, it attracted people from various backgrounds and was infamous for its licentious behavior.

The church in Corinth reflected this diversity, comprising Jews, Greeks, wealthy patrons, and poor laborers. This mix of backgrounds led to a dynamic but fractious community.

Paul founded the Corinthian church during his second missionary journey (Acts 18:1-17) and spent about 18 months there, teaching and establishing the new believers. However, after his departure, reports reached him of various issues arising within the church, prompting him to write 1 Corinthians to address these problems.

Issues in the Corinthian Church

The Corinthian church struggled with several significant issues, including divisions, immorality, lawsuits among believers, and misunderstandings about spiritual gifts and the resurrection. These problems were symptomatic of deeper spiritual immaturity and a lack of love and unity within the congregation.

1. Divisions and Factions: The church was plagued by factionalism, with members aligning themselves with different leaders—Paul, Apollos, Cephas, or Christ (1 Corinthians 1:10-13). This division undermined their unity and reflected a misunderstanding of Christian leadership and community.

2. Immorality: The church was also troubled by moral issues, including a case of incest (1 Corinthians 5:1-5) and general sexual immorality (1 Corinthians 6:12-20). Paul

admonished them to pursue holiness and to honor God with their bodies.

3. Lawsuits Among Believers: Members of the church were taking legal disputes against each other to secular courts, rather than resolving them within the Christian community (1 Corinthians 6:1-8). Paul urged them to seek reconciliation and to uphold the witness of the church.

4. Misunderstandings about Spiritual Gifts: The Corinthians were confused about the nature and purpose of spiritual gifts, leading to pride and competition rather than mutual edification (1 Corinthians 12-14). Paul emphasized that spiritual gifts should be exercised in love for the building up of the church.

5. The Resurrection: Some members doubted the resurrection of the dead, prompting Paul to provide a detailed defense of the resurrection and its significance for the Christian faith (1 Corinthians 15).

The Centrality of Love

In the midst of addressing these issues, Paul interjects his profound discourse on love in 1 Corinthians 13. This chapter serves as a corrective to the Corinthians' misguided priorities and behaviors. By placing love at the center of Christian life and practice, Paul provides a foundation upon which the church can build unity, holiness, and maturity.

1 Corinthians 13 is strategically positioned between chapters 12 and 14, which discuss spiritual gifts. Paul begins by acknowledging the diversity of gifts within the body of Christ but stresses that without love, these gifts are meaningless (1 Corinthians 12:31-13:3). He then elaborates on the nature and characteristics of love (1 Corinthians 13:4-7) before concluding with a reminder of love's enduring value (1 Corinthians 13:8-13).

The Characteristics of Love

In verses 4-7, Paul describes love in a series of positive and negative statements, painting a vivid picture of what true Christian love looks like. This love is patient and kind, not envious or boastful, not arrogant or rude. It does not insist on its own way, is not irritable or resentful, does not rejoice in wrongdoing but rejoices in the truth. Love bears all things, believes all things, hopes all things, endures all things.

These characteristics of love are a direct contrast to the behaviors and attitudes Paul addresses throughout the letter. The Corinthians' divisions, immorality, and misuse of spiritual gifts all stem from a lack of genuine love. By highlighting the attributes of love, Paul calls the Corinthians to a higher standard of relational and communal life.

Love as the Greatest Virtue

In the final verses of the chapter (1 Corinthians 13:8-13), Paul contrasts the temporary nature of spiritual gifts with the eternal nature of love. Prophecies, tongues, and knowledge will all pass away, but love will remain. He concludes by affirming that faith, hope, and love are the three enduring virtues of the Christian life, but the greatest of these is love.

This emphasis on love as the greatest virtue underscores its foundational importance in the Christian faith. For Paul, love is not merely an emotion or feeling but an active commitment to seek the good of others, reflecting the self-giving love of Christ. It is the defining characteristic of a true follower of Jesus and the essential ingredient for building a healthy, vibrant Christian community.

Practical Implications

Paul's discourse on love in 1 Corinthians 13 is not just a beautiful piece of literature but a practical guide for Christian living. It challenges believers to examine their own lives and relationships, asking whether they are characterized by the love Paul describes. It calls the church to prioritize love in all its activities, ensuring that everything is done for the edification and unity of the body of Christ.

In contemporary Christian living, Paul's theology of love remains as relevant as ever. Churches today continue to face divisions, moral challenges, and misunderstandings about spiritual gifts and practices. By returning to the foundational principles of love outlined in 1 Corinthians 13, believers can find a path toward greater unity, maturity, and faithfulness in their walk with Christ.

As we explore Paul's teachings on love in this book, may we be inspired to embody this love in our own lives and communities, reflecting the heart of the gospel and the character of our Savior?

The Characteristics of Love: A Detailed Exposition of 1 Corinthians 13:4-7

1 Corinthians 13:4-7 stands as one of the most beautiful and profound passages in the New Testament, providing a vivid and practical description of what love looks like in action. In these verses, Apostle Paul offers a series of positive and negative statements that paint a comprehensive picture of the characteristics of love. This chapter will delve into each of these attributes, unpacking their meanings and implications for Christian living.

1. Love is Patient

The Greek word used here, "makrothumei," implies a sense of enduring patience and long-suffering. It is the capacity to bear with others, to endure annoyances and difficulties without giving way to anger or despair. Patience is a fundamental aspect of love because it reflects God's patience with us. It allows relationships to flourish despite challenges and conflicts.

In practical terms, being patient means giving others time to grow and change, not rushing to judgment or action. It means holding space for people to express themselves and work through their struggles, showing the same patience God extends to us.

2. Love is Kind

Kindness, or "chresteuetai" in Greek, is an active expression of goodwill and benevolence. It goes beyond mere politeness to include tangible acts of care and compassion. Kindness is proactive; it seeks opportunities to serve and uplift others, often at a personal cost.

In a world where harshness and indifference are common, kindness stands out as a powerful testament to the transforming power of love. It involves simple acts like offering a listening ear, providing help without being asked, or speaking words of encouragement.

3. Love Does Not Envy

The term "zeloi" refers to jealousy or envy. Love does not begrudge others their blessings or successes. Envy stems from insecurity and a sense of competition, but love is secure and content, rejoicing in others' achievements and happiness.

When we are free from envy, we can genuinely celebrate the good things that happen to others. This creates a community where people feel supported and valued, knowing that their joys are shared rather than resented.

4. Love Does Not Boast

Boasting, or "perpereuetai," involves self-promotion and seeking to elevate oneself above others. Love is humble, recognizing that true value comes from God, not from personal achievements or status. It refrains from drawing attention to itself, focusing instead on uplifting others.

In practical terms, this means speaking in ways that honor others and give credit where it is due. It means resisting the temptation to make everything about oneself and instead shining a light on the contributions and qualities of those around us.

5. Love Is Not Arrogant

Arrogance, described by the Greek word "phusioutai," denotes a sense of inflated self-importance and superiority. Love is grounded in humility, acknowledging our own weaknesses and the value of others. It does not look down on others or assume an air of condescension.

Humility is central to love because it opens the way for genuine connection and mutual respect. It allows us to see others as equals, deserving of honor and dignity, regardless of their status or accomplishments.

6. Love Is Not Rude

Rudeness, or "aschemonei," involves behavior that is disrespectful or inconsiderate. Love is characterized by courtesy and respect, treating others with dignity and honor. It avoids actions and words that cause unnecessary offense or discomfort.

Practicing love in this way means being mindful of how our actions and words affect others. It involves being polite, considerate, and attentive to the needs and feelings of those around us.

7. Love Does Not Insist on Its Own Way

The phrase "ou zetei ta heautes" means that love is not self-seeking or selfish. It prioritizes the well-being and interests of others over its own desires. Love is willing to compromise, to give up its own preferences for the sake of others.

This selflessness is at the heart of Christian love. It mirrors the sacrificial love of Christ, who gave Himself up for us. In our relationships, this means being flexible, accommodating, and willing to put others' needs before our own.

8. Love Is Not Irritable

Irritability, or "paroxynetai," refers to being easily angered or provoked. Love maintains composure and emotional control, responding to provocations with grace and patience. It does not allow minor frustrations to disrupt its peace or harm its relationships.

In practice, this means developing a calm and forgiving demeanor. It involves letting go of minor annoyances and responding to difficulties with a gentle and patient spirit.

9. Love Is Not Resentful

The phrase "ou logizetai to kakon" literally means "does not count the wrongs." Love does not hold grudges or keep a record of wrongs. It is willing to forgive and move past offenses, not allowing bitterness to take root.

Forgiveness is a crucial aspect of love. It involves releasing past hurts and not allowing them to define the present or future of a relationship. This fosters an environment of grace and reconciliation.

10. Love Does Not Rejoice at Wrongdoing

Love does not take pleasure in unrighteousness or injustice. Instead, it rejoices with the truth ("sugchairei de te aletheia"). It finds joy in honesty, integrity, and justice. Love stands against evil and aligns itself with what is good and true.

In practical terms, this means being an advocate for truth and justice, celebrating what is right and standing against what is wrong. It means being honest and transparent in our dealings with others.

11. Love Bears All Things

The Greek word "stegō" implies covering, protecting, or enduring. Love is resilient and enduring, willing to bear hardships and challenges for the sake of others. It provides a protective and supportive presence.

In relationships, this means being a source of strength and support, standing by others in difficult times, and offering unwavering loyalty and commitment.

12. Love Believes All Things

This phrase, "panta pisteuei," means that love is trusting and believes the best in others. It is not cynical or suspicious but gives others the benefit of the doubt. Love has faith in people and in the transformative power of God.

Trust is a cornerstone of loving relationships. It means believing in others' potential and integrity, encouraging and affirming them in their journey.

13. Love Hopes All Things

The phrase "panta elpizei" means that love is hopeful, always looking forward with optimism and confidence in

God's promises. It maintains a positive outlook and expects the best outcomes.

Hope sustains love through difficult times. It means holding on to the belief that God is at work and that good will ultimately prevail.

14. Love Endures All Things

Finally, "panta hypomenei" means that love endures, perseveres, and remains steadfast in the face of trials. It does not give up or abandon others when times are tough. Love is characterized by its durability and constancy.

Endurance is the ultimate test of love. It involves remaining faithful and committed, even when it is difficult, costly, or painful.

Conclusion

The characteristics of love described by Paul in 1 Corinthians 13:4-7 provide a comprehensive and practical guide for Christian living. They challenge us to cultivate a love that is patient, kind, humble, and selfless, a love that forgives, trusts, hopes, and endures. This love, reflective of Christ's own love for us, is the foundation upon which a healthy, vibrant Christian community is built.

As we strive to embody these qualities in our own lives, we contribute to a culture of love that can transform relationships, churches, and ultimately, the world. May Paul's words inspire us to live out this love in all that we do, bearing witness to the power of the gospel and the reality of God's love in our lives.

Love as the Greatest Virtue: Why Paul Elevates Love Above Faith and Hope

In 1 Corinthians 13:13, Apostle Paul makes a profound statement: "And now these three remain: faith, hope, and love. But the greatest of these is love." This declaration elevates love above two other central Christian virtues—faith and hope. To fully grasp why Paul places such a premium on love, we must delve into the theological, practical, and relational reasons underlying this prioritization.

Understanding Faith, Hope, and Love

Before exploring why love is the greatest, it is essential to understand the significance of faith and hope within the Christian framework.

Faith is the foundation of the Christian life. It is the means by which believers are justified (Romans 5:1) and the substance of their relationship with God. Faith involves trust in God's promises, belief in His character, and reliance on His grace. Hebrews 11:1 defines faith as "the assurance of things hoped for, the conviction of things not seen."

Hope is the confident expectation of what God has promised. It is not mere wishful thinking but a firm assurance based on God's faithfulness. Hope sustains believers through trials and challenges, anchoring their souls in the certainty of God's future provision and the fulfillment of His promises (Hebrews 6:19).

Love, as Paul describes it, is an active, self-giving, and sacrificial force. It is not just an emotion but a commitment to seek the good of others, reflecting God's own love for humanity. Love is the fulfillment of the law (Romans 13:10) and the hallmark of true discipleship (John 13:35).

The Supremacy of Love

Paul's assertion that love is the greatest virtue can be understood through several key perspectives:

1. Love is Eternal

Unlike faith and hope, which pertain to our earthly and temporal experience, love is eternal. Faith will one day become sight, and hope will be realized in the fulfillment of God's promises. However, love will endure forever. In the new heavens and new earth, love will remain as the defining characteristic of our relationship with God and with one another.

1 Corinthians 13:8 states, "Love never ends. But as for prophecies, they will come to an end; as for tongues, they will cease; as for knowledge, it will come to an end." This permanence of love underscores its supremacy. When the

temporary gives way to the eternal, love continues, unbroken and unchanged.

2. Love Reflects God's Nature

God is love (1 John 4:8). Love is intrinsic to God's nature and character. While faith and hope are vital responses to God's revelation, love is a direct reflection of who God is. By elevating love above faith and hope, Paul aligns the believer's highest calling with the very essence of God.

When Christians love, they manifest the divine nature. This is why love fulfills the law—because the law is an expression of God's righteous and loving character. Love, therefore, is not just a virtue among others but the very essence of godliness.

3. Love is the Fulfillment of the Law

Paul writes in Romans 13:10, "Love does no harm to a neighbor. Therefore, love is the fulfillment of the law." The entire moral law is encapsulated in the command to love God and love our neighbor (Matthew 22:37-40). This fulfillment highlights the comprehensive nature of love. It encompasses all ethical and moral directives and provides the motive and power to obey them.

Where faith and hope orient us towards God, love extends both vertically (towards God) and horizontally (towards others). It encapsulates the whole duty of humanity, ensuring that our actions align with God's will and purpose.

4. Love is the Evidence of Faith and Hope

Genuine faith and hope inevitably produce love. James 2:17 reminds us that faith without works is dead, and Galatians 5:6 emphasizes that "the only thing that counts is faith expressing itself through love." Similarly, hope inspires and sustains love, as seen in Colossians 1:4-5, where Paul commends the Colossians for their love "because of the hope stored up for you in heaven."

Love is the tangible evidence of a living faith and a vibrant hope. It is the fruit that proves the root. Without love, faith and hope remain abstract and unproven.

5. Love is the Greatest Witness

In John 13:35, Jesus states, "By this everyone will know that you are my disciples if you love one another." Love is the primary witness to the world of the reality of Christ. While faith is personal and hope is often internal, love is outward and visible. It is the defining mark of Christian community and the most potent testimony to the transformative power of the gospel.

When the world sees genuine love in action, it encounters the reality of God. This witness is irreplaceable and essential for the mission of the church.

Practical Implications for Christian Living

Understanding why love is the greatest virtue has profound implications for how Christians live out their faith:

1. Prioritizing Relationships: Christians are called to prioritize relationships over rituals, and people over programs. Love should govern all interactions and decisions, ensuring that actions are motivated by genuine care and concern for others.

2. Embracing Sacrifice: Love often requires sacrifice, putting others' needs ahead of one's own. This sacrificial love mirrors Christ's own sacrifice and is a powerful demonstration of faith in action.

3. Cultivating Community: A community built on love is marked by unity, support, and mutual encouragement. Christians are called to foster environments where love can flourish, breaking down barriers and building bridges of understanding and cooperation.

4. Witnessing through Love: The greatest evangelistic tool is a life characterized by love. As believers live out the love of Christ, they draw others to the faith and provide a compelling witness to the world.

5. Pursuing Holiness: Love is intrinsically linked to holiness. It seeks the good of others and aligns with God's

righteous standards. Christians are called to pursue a holy life, motivated by love for God and neighbor.

Conclusion

Paul's elevation of love above faith and hope is not a dismissal of these crucial virtues but a recognition of love's unique and enduring nature. Love is eternal, reflecting God's very essence and fulfilling the law. It is the evidence of genuine faith and hope and the greatest witness to the world of the reality of Christ.

As believers strive to live out Paul's teachings, they are called to cultivate a love that is patient, kind, humble, and selfless—a love that bears all things, believes all things, hopes all things, and endures all things. This love is the foundation upon which a vibrant and faithful Christian life is built, and it is the greatest virtue that we are called to embody.

By prioritizing love in our lives, we fulfill our highest calling, reflect God's nature, and provide a powerful testimony to the world. In this way, we align with Paul's profound declaration: "The greatest of these is love."

CHAPTER 02

LOVE AND THE LAW

Romans 13:8-10: Love Fulfills the Law

In his letter to the Romans, Apostle Paul presents a compelling argument that love is the fulfillment of the law. Romans 13:8-10 encapsulates this profound theological insight: "Owe no one anything, except to love each other, for the one who loves another has fulfilled the law. For the commandments, 'You shall not commit adultery, You shall not murder, You shall not steal, You shall not covet,' and any other commandment, are summed up in this word: 'You shall love your neighbor as yourself.' Love does no wrong to a neighbor; therefore love is the fulfilling of the law." This chapter will explore Paul's view of the law, the transition from the Old Covenant to the New Covenant, and how love serves as the ultimate fulfillment of God's commandments.

Paul's View of the Law

To understand Paul's assertion that love fulfills the law, it is essential to grasp his broader perspective on the law. Paul, a former Pharisee, had a deep and nuanced understanding of the Mosaic Law. His epistles reflect a transformation in his thinking about the law's role in light of Christ's life, death, and resurrection.

The Purpose of the Law

Paul saw the law as holy, righteous, and good (Romans 7:12). It was given by God to reveal His character and to set apart the people of Israel as His covenant community. The law provided moral and ceremonial guidelines intended to guide Israel in righteous living and worship.

However, Paul also recognized that the law had a secondary purpose: to reveal sin and humanity's inability to achieve righteousness through their own efforts. In Romans 3:20, he states, "For by works of the law no human being will be justified in his sight, since through the law comes knowledge of sin." The law highlighted humanity's need for a savior.

The Old Covenant and Its Limitations

Under the Old Covenant, the law served as a tutor or guardian, guiding the people until the coming of Christ (Galatians 3:24). It required strict adherence to numerous commandments and rituals, but it could not provide the power to overcome sin. The sacrificial system temporarily addressed sin but could not cleanse the conscience fully or change the heart.

Paul understood that the law, while good, was limited because it depended on the human ability to comply. Its ultimate purpose was to lead people to Christ, who would fulfill the law and provide a new way of righteousness through faith.

The Transition from the Old Covenant to the New Covenant

With the advent of Jesus Christ, a significant transition occurred—from the Old Covenant, based on the law, to the New Covenant, grounded in grace and truth (John 1:17).

Christ Fulfills the Law

Jesus declared in Matthew 5:17, "Do not think that I have come to abolish the Law or the Prophets; I have not come to abolish them but to fulfill them." Christ fulfilled the law in several ways:

- Perfect Obedience: Jesus perfectly obeyed the moral, ceremonial, and judicial aspects of the law, living a sinless life.

- Atoning Sacrifice: Through His death on the cross, Jesus fulfilled the sacrificial system, offering Himself as the once-for-all sacrifice for sin (Hebrews 10:10).

- Mediation of a New Covenant: Jesus established the New Covenant through His blood, providing a way for believers to be justified by faith and empowered by the Holy Spirit to live righteously (Luke 22:20).

The Law Written on Hearts

Under the New Covenant, the external requirements of the law are internalized. Jeremiah prophesied this transformation: "I will put my law within them, and I will write it on their hearts. And I will be their God, and they shall be my people" (Jeremiah 31:33). Paul echoes this in Romans 8:3-4, explaining that what the law could not do, weakened by the flesh, God did by sending His Son. The righteous requirement of the law is fulfilled in those who walk according to the Spirit.

The New Covenant emphasizes an inward change, where believers are given a new heart and spirit, enabling them to live out the principles of the law through the power of love.

Love as the Fulfillment of the Law

Paul's statement in Romans 13:8-10 that love fulfills the law is rooted in Jesus' teaching and the transformative power of the New Covenant.

The Command to Love

Jesus summarized the law with two great commandments: "You shall love the Lord your God with all your heart and with all your soul and with all your mind" and "You shall love your neighbor as yourself" (Matthew 22:37-39). All the Law and the Prophets hang on these two commandments.

Paul reiterates this summary, emphasizing that love for one's neighbor encapsulates the moral directives of the law. When believers love their neighbors genuinely, they naturally fulfill the commandments regarding how to treat others—adultery, murder, theft, and covetousness are all precluded by love.

Love Does No Harm

Paul highlights that "love does no wrong to a neighbor" (Romans 13:10). This principle is foundational because it moves beyond mere avoidance of wrongdoing to the proactive pursuit of others' well-being. Love seeks the good of others, ensuring that one's actions are beneficial rather than harmful.

This positive ethic transforms the law from a set of prohibitions to a dynamic force for good. Love motivates believers to act justly, compassionately, and righteously, fulfilling the law's true intent.

The Empowering of the Spirit

Under the New Covenant, believers are indwelt by the Holy Spirit, who produces the fruit of love (Galatians 5:22-23). This divine empowerment enables Christians to live out the law's requirements in a way that was impossible under the Old Covenant.

The Spirit guides and empowers believers to love authentically, moving beyond external compliance to a heartfelt devotion to God and others. This transformation is the hallmark of the New Covenant and the fulfillment of the law through love.

Conclusion

Paul's teaching in Romans 13:8-10 encapsulates a profound truth: love fulfills the law. This fulfillment is rooted in the transition from the Old Covenant, with its external requirements and limitations, to the New Covenant, where the law is internalized and empowered by the Holy Spirit.

Love, as the greatest virtue, reflects God's nature, fulfills His commandments, and provides the ultimate evidence of faith and hope. It is the dynamic force that transforms relationships, communities, and the world, embodying the very essence of the gospel.

As believers live out this love, they fulfill the law in its truest sense, demonstrating the reality of Christ's transformative work and bearing witness to the power of the

New Covenant. In this way, Paul's declaration that love is the fulfillment of the law becomes a practical and powerful guide for Christian living.

The Command to Love: How Love Summarizes and Fulfills the Ten Commandments

In his letter to the Romans, Apostle Paul encapsulates the essence of the Mosaic Law in one profound statement: "Love does no wrong to a neighbor; therefore love is the fulfilling of the law" (Romans 13:10). This chapter will explore how love summarizes and fulfills the Ten Commandments, transforming them from a list of prohibitions into a dynamic, life-giving force that shapes the Christian life.

The Ten Commandments: An Overview

The Ten Commandments, given to Moses on Mount Sinai, form the cornerstone of the Old Covenant. They are divided into two sections: the first four commandments focus on the relationship between humanity and God, while the last six address interpersonal relationships. Together, they provide a comprehensive moral framework for God's people.

The First Four Commandments: Loving God

1. You shall have no other gods before Me.

2. You shall not make for yourself a carved image...

3. You shall not take the name of the Lord your God in vain.

4. Remember the Sabbath day, to keep it holy.

The Last Six Commandments: Loving Neighbor

5. Honor your father and your mother.

6. You shall not murder.

7. You shall not commit adultery.

8. You shall not steal.

9. You shall not bear false witness against your neighbor.

10. You shall not covet.

Jesus' Summary of the Law

Jesus, when asked about the greatest commandment, provided a summary that encapsulates the entire law: "You shall love the Lord your God with all your heart and with all your soul and with all your mind. This is the great and first commandment. And a second is like it: You shall love your neighbor as yourself. On these two commandments depend all the Law and the Prophets" (Matthew 22:37-40).

In these words, Jesus reveals that love is the underlying principle of the law. Love for God and love for neighbor are the two hinges upon which the entire law turns. Paul's teaching in Romans 13:8-10 echoes this summary, emphasizing that love fulfills the law.

Love Summarizes the Commandments

1. Love for God

The first four commandments are centered on our relationship with God. When we love God with all our heart, soul, and mind, we naturally fulfill these commandments.

1. No Other Gods: Loving God supremely means that we acknowledge Him as the only true God, giving Him the highest place in our hearts and lives.

2. No Idols: Love for God leads us to worship Him in spirit and truth, avoiding any form of idolatry that diminishes His glory.

3. Honoring God's Name: When we love God, we honor His name in our speech and conduct, avoiding misuse and upholding its sanctity.

4. Keeping the Sabbath: Love for God includes honoring His creation and redemption, dedicating time for rest and worship, and reflecting on His goodness and grace.

2. Love for Neighbor

The last six commandments focus on our relationships with others. Love for our neighbor ensures that we naturally fulfill these commandments.

5. Honor Parents: Love for others begins at home, respecting and honoring our parents, and recognizing their role in our lives.

6. Do Not Murder: Love values and preserves life, rejecting hatred, anger, and violence that lead to harm.

7. Do Not Commit Adultery: Love respects the sanctity of marriage, upholding fidelity and purity in relationships.

8. Do Not Steal: Love respects others' property and rights, promoting honesty and integrity.

9. Do Not Bear False Witness: Love values truth and seeks to protect others' reputations, avoiding lies and deceit.

10. Do Not Covet: Love fosters contentment and gratitude, rejecting envy and greed that disrupt peace and harmony.

Love Fulfills the Commandments

Paul's assertion that love fulfills the law goes beyond merely summarizing it; he suggests that love brings the law to its intended completion. When we love as Christ loves, we fulfill the righteous requirements of the law in a way that external adherence alone cannot achieve.

The Transformative Power of Love

Love transforms obedience from a duty to a delight. Under the Old Covenant, the law was an external set of rules that people struggled to keep. Under the New Covenant, love internalizes these principles, making them a natural outflow of a heart transformed by grace.

1. Internalization: The Holy Spirit writes God's laws on our hearts (Hebrews 8:10). This internalization means that

obedience is no longer about external conformity but about inward transformation.

2. Empowerment: The Spirit empowers believers to love genuinely and sacrificially, fulfilling the law's demands through the power of love (Galatians 5:22-23).

3. Motivation: Love as the motivation for obedience ensures that our actions are sincere and aligned with God's will, moving beyond legalism to genuine righteousness.

Practical Implications of Love

Understanding that love fulfills the law has practical implications for how we live out our faith.

1. Holistic Obedience: Love leads to holistic obedience, where every aspect of our lives—thoughts, words, and actions—aligns with God's commandments.

2. Relational Focus: Love shifts the focus from rule-keeping to relationship-building, prioritizing healthy, godly relationships with God and others.

3. Ethical Living: Love guides ethical decision-making, ensuring that our choices reflect God's character and honor His commandments.

Examples of Love in Action

1. In the Church: Love fosters unity and mutual edification within the body of Christ. It encourages believers

to serve one another, bear each other's burdens, and build up the community in love (Ephesians 4:1-3, 16).

2. In the Family: Love strengthens family bonds, promoting respect, care, and support among family members. It ensures that homes are places of nurture and godly influence (Colossians 3:18-21).

3. In Society: Love inspires believers to seek justice, mercy, and peace in society. It motivates them to stand against injustice, help the marginalized, and promote the common good (Micah 6:8, Matthew 25:35-40).

Conclusion

Paul's teaching in Romans 13:8-10 reveals a profound truth: love is the fulfillment of the law. By summarizing and internalizing the Ten Commandments, love transforms legalistic adherence into joyful, Spirit-empowered obedience. This love, grounded in the greatest commandments given by Jesus, calls believers to a life that honors God and blesses others.

As we embrace the command to love, we fulfill the law's true intent, reflecting God's character and advancing His kingdom on earth. Love becomes the guiding principle for all our actions, relationships, and decisions, ensuring that our lives align with God's perfect will.

In this way, Paul's declaration that love fulfills the law is not just a theological concept but a practical and powerful guide for Christian living. By prioritizing love, we honor God's commandments, build up His church, and witness to the world of the transforming power of His grace.

Practical Implications: Living Out Love in Daily Interactions and Community Life

In his letter to the Romans, Apostle Paul emphasizes that love is the fulfillment of the law. This profound truth has far-reaching practical implications for daily interactions and community life. As we explore these implications, we will see how living out love transforms our relationships, guides our actions, and shapes our communities according to the principles of the New Covenant.

Understanding the Command to Love

Paul's statement in Romans 13:8-10 that "love is the fulfilling of the law" challenges believers to move beyond a superficial understanding of love to a deep, transformative practice. Love, according to Paul, is not merely an emotion but an active commitment to seek the good of others, grounded in the example and teachings of Jesus Christ.

Key Elements of Love

1. Selflessness: True love puts others' needs and well-being above one's own.

2. Sacrifice: Love often requires personal sacrifice, mirroring the sacrificial love of Christ.

3. Empathy: Love involves understanding and sharing in the feelings of others, leading to compassionate action.

4. Forgiveness: Love forgives offenses and seeks reconciliation, promoting peace and unity.

Living Out Love in Daily Interactions

Love is most effectively demonstrated in the ordinary, everyday moments of life. It influences how we treat others in our families, workplaces, neighborhoods, and churches.

In the Family

1. Spousal Relationships: Love in marriage involves mutual respect, selfless service, and unwavering commitment. Paul's exhortation to husbands and wives in Ephesians 5:22-33 highlights the self-giving love that mirrors Christ's relationship with the church.

2. Parent-Child Relationships: Parents are called to nurture and instruct their children in love, avoiding harshness and fostering a supportive environment (Colossians 3:21). Children, in turn, are to honor and obey their parents, reflecting a loving family dynamic.

3. Extended Family: Love extends to caring for elderly parents and supporting extended family members,

emphasizing the importance of familial bonds and responsibilities.

In the Workplace

1. Ethical Conduct: Love guides ethical behavior in the workplace, promoting honesty, integrity, and fairness. It involves treating colleagues and subordinates with respect and dignity, valuing their contributions.

2. Service Orientation: Viewing work as an opportunity to serve others rather than merely a means of personal gain transforms workplace interactions. Colossians 3:23-24 encourages believers to work heartily as for the Lord, embodying love in their professional lives.

3. Conflict Resolution: Love fosters a cooperative and harmonious work environment, encouraging constructive dialogue and peaceful resolution of conflicts.

In the Neighborhood

1. Community Involvement: Love motivates active participation in local communities, seeking to contribute positively and support communal well-being.

2. Hospitality: Practicing hospitality, as instructed in Romans 12:13, involves welcoming neighbors and strangers, creating a sense of belonging and community.

3. Acts of Kindness: Simple acts of kindness, such as helping a neighbor in need or offering a listening ear, reflect the love of Christ in everyday interactions.

In the Church

1. Unity and Edification: Love is the glue that holds the church together, promoting unity and mutual edification. Ephesians 4:1-3 calls believers to maintain the unity of the Spirit in the bond of peace, while 1 Corinthians 12:25-26 emphasizes the importance of caring for one another within the body of Christ.

2. Service and Ministry: Love drives believers to serve one another through various ministries, using their gifts for the common good (1 Peter 4:10). This service is motivated by genuine care and a desire to build up the church.

3. Discipleship and Encouragement: Loving one another involves disciplining and encouraging fellow believers in their faith journeys. This includes offering support, accountability, and spiritual guidance.

Living Out Love in Community Life

Love extends beyond individual interactions to shape the broader community. It influences social justice, public policy, and communal values.

Social Justice

1. Advocacy for the Marginalized: Love compels believers to advocate for the marginalized and oppressed, seeking justice and equity. Proverbs 31:8-9 urges us to speak up for those who cannot speak for themselves and defend the rights of the poor and needy.

2. Compassionate Outreach: Engaging in compassionate outreach to those in need, such as the homeless, refugees, and victims of injustice, demonstrates Christ-like love. Matthew 25:35-40 emphasizes that serving the least of these is serving Christ Himself.

Public Policy

1. Promoting the Common Good: Love influences how Christians engage in public policy, advocating for laws and policies that promote the common good and protect human dignity.

2. Civil Discourse: Love guides believers to engage in civil discourse, treating others with respect even in disagreement, and seeking constructive solutions to societal issues.

Communal Values

1. Creating Inclusive Communities: Love fosters inclusive communities where all individuals are valued and accepted, regardless of background or status. James 2:1-9

warns against showing favoritism, calling for equal treatment of all people.

2. Encouraging Volunteerism: Encouraging volunteerism and community service as expressions of love helps build strong, caring communities. This involves organizing and participating in community service projects and initiatives.

Overcoming Challenges to Living Out Love

Living out love in daily interactions and community life is not without challenges. However, believers are equipped and empowered by the Holy Spirit to overcome these obstacles.

Dealing with Conflict

1. Pursuing Reconciliation: Love seeks reconciliation in conflict situations, promoting forgiveness and understanding. Matthew 18:15-17 provides a process for addressing conflicts within the church, emphasizing the goal of restoration.

2. Practicing Patience: Patience is crucial in dealing with difficult people and situations. Love requires enduring patience, reflecting God's patience with us (1 Corinthians 13:4).

Addressing Selfishness

1. Cultivating Humility: Love involves humility, putting others' needs above our own. Philippians 2:3-4 encourages believers to consider others better than themselves and look to others' interests.

2. Sacrificial Giving: Love often requires sacrificial giving, whether of time, resources, or energy. This reflects Christ's sacrificial love for us (John 15:13).

Overcoming Fear

1. Trusting God's Provision: Fear of scarcity can hinder loving actions. Trusting in God's provision frees believers to give generously and love fearlessly (Matthew 6:25-34).

2. Boldness in Love: The Holy Spirit empowers believers with boldness to love in challenging circumstances. 2 Timothy 1:7 reminds us that God has given us a spirit not of fear but of power, love, and self-control.

Conclusion

Paul's teaching that love fulfills the law has profound practical implications for daily interactions and community life. By embodying selfless, sacrificial, empathetic, and forgiving love, believers transform their relationships and communities, reflecting the heart of the gospel.

Living out love in daily interactions involves practical steps within families, workplaces, neighborhoods, and churches. It also extends to broader community engagement, influencing social justice, public policy, and communal values. Overcoming challenges to living out love requires reliance on the Holy Spirit, patience, humility, and boldness.

As believers strive to live out this love, they fulfill the law's true intent, demonstrating the reality of Christ's transformative work and bearing witness to the power of the New Covenant. In this way, Paul's declaration that love is the fulfillment of the law becomes a practical and powerful guide for Christian living, shaping individuals and communities according to God's perfect will.

CHAPTER 03

LOVE AND CHRISTIAN FREEDOM

Galatians 5:13-14: Freedom to Love

In his letter to the Galatians, Apostle Paul addresses the concept of Christian freedom, emphasizing that it is not a license for self-indulgence but an opportunity to serve one another in love. Galatians 5:13-14 states, "You, my brothers and sisters, were called to be free. But do not use your freedom to indulge the flesh; rather, serve one another humbly in love. For the entire law is fulfilled in keeping this one command: 'Love your neighbor as yourself.'" This chapter will explore the balance between liberty and responsibility in Christian freedom and how love is central to this balance.

Understanding Freedom in Christ

Christian freedom is a central theme in Paul's letters. It represents the liberation from the bondage of sin and the law, achieved through faith in Jesus Christ. However, this freedom is not an end in itself but a means to live out God's purposes, primarily through love.

The Nature of Christian Freedom

1. Liberation from Sin: Through Christ, believers are set free from the power of sin. Romans 6:18 states, "You have been set free from sin and have become slaves to righteousness." This freedom allows believers to live a life pleasing to God, no longer dominated by sinful desires.

2. Freedom from the Law: Christians are no longer under the Mosaic Law's requirements as a means of justification. Galatians 5:1 proclaims, "It is for freedom that Christ has set us free. Stand firm, then, and do not let yourselves be burdened again by a yoke of slavery." This freedom means that believers are justified by faith in Christ, not by adherence to the law.

3. Freedom to Serve: Paul emphasizes that Christian freedom is not for self-indulgence but for serving others in love. This service reflects the selfless love of Christ and fulfills the law's true intent.

The Balance Between Liberty and Responsibility

While Christian freedom liberates believers from the constraints of the law and sin, it also carries a responsibility to live in a manner that honors God and serves others. This balance between liberty and responsibility is crucial for a healthy Christian life.

Misuse of Freedom

1. Indulgence of the Flesh: Paul warns against using freedom as an excuse to indulge the flesh—our sinful nature. Galatians 5:13 cautions, "Do not use your freedom to indulge the flesh." Indulgence in the flesh leads to behaviors that are contrary to God's will and destructive to relationships.

2. Anarchy and Selfishness: Without the guiding principle of love, freedom can devolve into anarchy and selfishness, where individuals pursue their desires at the expense of others' well-being. This misuse of freedom undermines the community and hinders spiritual growth.

Responsible Use of Freedom

1. Serving Others in Love: The proper use of Christian freedom involves serving others humbly in love. This service reflects the example of Christ, who came not to be served but to serve (Mark 10:45). Serving others in love fulfills the law's requirements and builds up the body of Christ.

2. Fulfilling the Law: Paul states that "the entire law is fulfilled in keeping this one command: 'Love your neighbor

as yourself'" (Galatians 5:14). This fulfillment highlights that true freedom leads to living out God's commandments through love, ensuring that our actions align with His will.

3. Walking by the Spirit: Responsible use of freedom involves walking by the Spirit, allowing Him to guide our actions and decisions. Galatians 5:16 encourages believers to "walk by the Spirit, and you will not gratify the desires of the flesh." The Spirit empowers believers to live in love, joy, peace, and other fruits that reflect a life pleasing to God.

Love as the Fulfillment of Freedom

Love is the central principle that ensures Christian freedom is used responsibly. It transforms freedom from a self-centered pursuit into a Christ-centered service.

The Role of Love in Christian Freedom

1. Motivating Service: Love motivates believers to serve others selflessly. This service is not out of obligation but out of genuine care and compassion. Love seeks the best for others, ensuring that our freedom benefits those around us.

2. Building Community: Love fosters a sense of community and mutual support. It encourages believers to bear each other's burdens, promote unity, and build up the church. This communal aspect of love ensures that freedom strengthens the body of Christ rather than causing division.

3. Reflecting Christ: Love reflects the character of Christ, who used His freedom to serve and sacrifice for others. By loving others as Christ loves us, believers fulfill their calling and witness to the transformative power of the gospel.

Practical Expressions of Love in Freedom

1. Acts of Kindness: Simple acts of kindness, such as helping a neighbor, offering encouragement, or providing for someone in need, are practical expressions of love. These acts demonstrate that freedom is used to uplift others.

2. Volunteering and Service: Engaging in volunteer work and community service projects allows believers to use their freedom to make a positive impact. This service can include helping in local charities, church ministries, or social justice initiatives.

3. Advocacy and Justice: Love motivates believers to advocate for justice and equality, standing up for the marginalized and oppressed. This advocacy reflects God's heart for justice and uses freedom to promote the common good.

4. Discipleship and Mentorship: Investing in the spiritual growth of others through discipleship and mentorship is a powerful expression of love. This

commitment helps others grow in their faith and use their freedom responsibly.

Overcoming Challenges in Living Out Freedom with Love

Living out Christian freedom with love is not without challenges. However, believers are equipped by the Holy Spirit to navigate these challenges and remain faithful to their calling.

Dealing with Legalism

1. Embracing Grace: Legalism, the strict adherence to the law as a means of justification undermines the freedom found in Christ. Believers must embrace grace, recognizing that justification comes through faith in Christ alone (Ephesians 2:8-9).

2. Avoiding Judgmental Attitudes: Legalism often leads to judgmental attitudes and division. Love calls believers to avoid judging others based on their adherence to the law and instead focus on mutual edification and support (Romans 14:1-4).

Navigating Libertinism

1. Setting Boundaries: While Christian freedom allows for liberty, it also requires boundaries to prevent indulgence in sinful behaviors. Setting personal and communal

boundaries helps believers live in a manner that honors God (1 Corinthians 6:12).

2. Seeking Accountability: Accountability within the Christian community is essential for maintaining the responsible use of freedom. Believers should seek relationships that provide encouragement, correction, and support in living out their faith.

Conclusion

Paul's teaching in Galatians 5:13-14 provides a profound understanding of Christian freedom. This freedom, achieved through faith in Christ, liberates believers from the bondage of sin and the law. However, it also carries the responsibility to live out this freedom in love.

Balancing liberty and responsibility is crucial for a healthy Christian life. Love serves as the guiding principle that ensures freedom is used not for self-indulgence but for serving others and fulfilling God's commandments. By walking by the Spirit and embracing the transformative power of love, believers can navigate the challenges of legalism and libertinism, using their freedom to build up the body of Christ and witness to the world.

As believers strive to live out their freedom with love, they fulfill the law's true intent and reflect the heart of the gospel. This responsible use of freedom transforms daily interactions and community life, ensuring that Christian freedom is a powerful force for good in the world.

Love as Service: Using Freedom to Serve One Another in Love

In his letter to the Galatians, Apostle Paul provides a profound understanding of Christian freedom, emphasizing that this freedom is not for self-indulgence but for serving one another in love. Galatians 5:13-14 states, "You, my brothers and sisters, were called to be free. But do not use your freedom to indulge the flesh; rather, serve one another humbly in love. For the entire law is fulfilled in keeping this one command: 'Love your neighbor as yourself.'" This chapter explores how love manifests as service and how Christian freedom empowers believers to serve others selflessly.

The Concept of Christian Freedom

Christian freedom, as taught by Paul, is liberation from the bondage of sin and the law, achieved through faith in Jesus Christ. This freedom is not an excuse for self-indulgence but a call to a higher purpose—serving others in love.

Liberation from Sin and the Law

1. Freedom from Sin: Through Christ's sacrifice, believers are set free from the power of sin. Romans 6:18 says,

"You have been set free from sin and have become slaves to righteousness." This freedom enables believers to live righteously, no longer dominated by sinful desires.

2. Freedom from the Law: Christians are no longer under the Mosaic Law's requirements for justification. Galatians 5:1 declares, "It is for freedom that Christ has set us free. Stand firm, then, and do not let yourselves be burdened again by a yoke of slavery." This freedom means justification comes through faith in Christ, not through law-keeping.

The Purpose of Freedom

Paul emphasizes that the purpose of Christian freedom is not self-indulgence but service. Freedom in Christ is a call to love and serve others, reflecting the love of Christ.

Love as Service

Love, according to Paul, is the driving force behind true Christian service. It transforms freedom from a self-centered pursuit into a Christ-centered service.

The Example of Jesus

Jesus Christ is the ultimate example of love as service. He came not to be served but to serve and to give His life as a ransom for many (Mark 10:45). His entire ministry was characterized by selfless service, culminating in His sacrificial death on the cross.

1. Selfless Service: Jesus demonstrated selfless service by healing the sick, feeding the hungry, and teaching the multitudes. He served others without seeking anything in return, motivated purely by love.

2. Sacrificial Love: Jesus' ultimate act of service was His sacrificial death. He laid down His life for humanity, offering Himself as the atoning sacrifice for our sins (John 15:13).

Serving One Another in Love

Paul calls believers to follow Jesus' example by using their freedom to serve one another in love. This service is not about seeking recognition or reward but about humbly putting others' needs above our own.

1. Humility in Service:

- Putting Others First: Serving in love means considering others' needs and interests above our own. Philippians 2:3-4 instructs, "Do nothing out of selfish ambition or vain conceit. Rather, in humility value others above yourselves, not looking to your own interests but each of you to the interests of the others."

- Selfless Actions: True service involves selfless actions that benefit others, whether through acts of kindness, support, or sacrifice. It means giving of our time, resources, and energy to help those in need.

2. Practical Expressions of Love through Service:

- Acts of Kindness: Simple acts of kindness, such as helping a neighbor, offering encouragement, or providing for someone's needs, reflect the love of Christ. These acts demonstrate that our freedom is used to uplift and support others.

- Volunteering and Community Service: Engaging in volunteer work and community service projects allows believers to use their freedom to make a positive impact. This service can include helping in local charities, church ministries, or social justice initiatives.

- Discipleship and Mentorship: Investing in the spiritual growth of others through discipleship and mentorship is a powerful expression of love. This commitment helps others grow in their faith and use their freedom responsibly.

- Advocacy and Justice: Love motivates believers to advocate for justice and equality, standing up for the marginalized and oppressed. This advocacy reflects God's heart for justice and uses freedom to promote the common good.

The Impact of Love as Service on the Community

When believers use their freedom to serve one another in love, it has a transformative impact on the community. Love as service builds a strong, supportive, and unified community that reflects the kingdom of God.

Building a Strong Community

1. Fostering Unity:

- Mutual Support: Serving one another in love fosters a sense of mutual support and solidarity. It creates an environment where individuals feel valued and cared for, promoting unity within the community.

- Breaking Down Barriers: Love as service breaks down barriers of division, whether based on race, class, or social status. It promotes inclusivity and equality, reflecting the inclusive nature of God's love.

2. Encouraging Growth:

- Spiritual Growth: Serving others in love encourages spiritual growth and maturity. It helps believers develop Christ-like character and deepens their relationship with God.

- Emotional Growth: Acts of service promote emotional well-being, both for those serving and those being served. It creates a supportive environment where individuals can thrive emotionally and mentally.

3. Demonstrating the Gospel:

- Witness to the World: A community characterized by love and service is a powerful witness to the world. It demonstrates the reality of the gospel and the transformative power of Christ's love.

- Reflecting Christ's Love: Serving in love reflects the love of Christ to those outside the community, drawing others to the faith and expanding God's kingdom.

Overcoming Challenges to Serving in Love

Living out love as service is not without challenges. However, believers are equipped by the Holy Spirit to navigate these challenges and remain faithful to their calling.

Dealing with Selfishness

1. Cultivating Humility:

- Embracing Humility: Overcoming selfishness requires cultivating humility, recognizing our dependence on God, and valuing others above ourselves.

- Daily Self-Examination: Regular self-examination and repentance help believers identify and address selfish tendencies, allowing them to serve more selflessly.

2. Seeking Accountability:

- Accountability Partners: Seeking accountability from fellow believers helps maintain a focus on selfless service. Accountability partners can provide encouragement, correction, and support in living out love as service.

Addressing Burnout

1. Finding Balance:

- Setting Boundaries: Setting healthy boundaries ensures that believers do not overextend themselves, leading to burnout. It is important to balance service with rest and self-care.

- Delegating Responsibilities: Sharing responsibilities within the community helps prevent burnout and ensures that the burden of service is distributed.

2. Seeking Renewal:

- Spiritual Renewal: Regular times of prayer, worship, and reflection renew the spirit and provide strength for continued service. Connecting with God is essential for sustaining a heart of service.

- Community Support: Receiving support from the community, whether through encouragement, prayer, or practical help, renews and strengthens those serving.

Conclusion

Paul's teaching in Galatians 5:13-14 provides a profound understanding of Christian freedom. This freedom, achieved through faith in Christ, liberates believers from the bondage of sin and the law. However, it also carries the responsibility to use this freedom to serve one another in love.

Love as service transforms freedom from a self-centered pursuit into a Christ-centered service. By following

Jesus' example and using their freedom to serve others, believers fulfill the law's true intent and reflect the heart of the gospel.

Living out love as service has a transformative impact on the community, fostering unity, encouraging growth, and demonstrating the gospel to the world. Overcoming challenges to serving in love requires humility, accountability, balance, and spiritual renewal.

As believers strive to live out their freedom by serving one another in love, they fulfill their calling and witness to the world of the transformative power of God's love. In this way, Paul's declaration that love fulfills the law becomes a practical and powerful guide for Christian living, shaping individuals and communities according to God's perfect will.

Contrasting Works of the Flesh and Fruit of the Spirit: The Centrality of Love in the Fruit of the Spirit

In his letter to the Galatians, Apostle Paul contrasts the works of the flesh with the fruit of the Spirit, emphasizing the transformative power of the Holy Spirit in the lives of believers. Galatians 5:19-23 provides a stark comparison between the destructive behaviors driven by the flesh and the life-giving virtues produced by the Spirit. At the heart of the fruit of the Spirit is love, which serves as the foundation for all other virtues. This chapter explores this contrast and highlights the centrality of love in the fruit of the Spirit.

The Works of the Flesh

Paul begins by listing the works of the flesh, and behaviors that result from living according to our sinful nature. These works are evident in their destructiveness and opposition to God's will.

Characteristics of the Works of the Flesh

1. Immorality and Impurity:

- Sexual Immorality: This includes any sexual behavior outside the bounds of God's design for marriage.

- Impurity and Debauchery: These terms encompass a range of morally corrupt and hedonistic behaviors that defile the body and mind.

2. Idolatry and Sorcery:

- Idolatry: Placing anything or anyone above God in our lives, whether it be material possessions, relationships, or ambitions.

- Sorcery: Engaging in occult practices or relying on supernatural powers apart from God.

3. Relational Sins:

- Enmity and Strife: Hostility and conflict that disrupt relationships and communities.

- Jealousy and Fits of Anger: Emotions that lead to destructive behavior and broken relationships.

- Rivalries, Dissensions, and Divisions: Competitive and divisive attitudes that fracture unity within the body of Christ.

4. Sins of Excess:

- Drunkenness and Orgies: Overindulgence in alcohol and other substances, as well as participating in wild, uncontrolled parties.

Consequences of the Works of the Flesh

Paul warns that those who practice such behaviors will not inherit the kingdom of God (Galatians 5:21). These works of the flesh lead to spiritual death, separation from God, and the breakdown of relationships and communities. They represent a life lived apart from the transformative power of the Holy Spirit.

The Fruit of the Spirit

In contrast to the works of the flesh, Paul presents the fruit of the Spirit, the virtues that the Holy Spirit produces in the lives of believers. These qualities reflect the character of Christ and are the evidence of a life transformed by God's Spirit.

Characteristics of the Fruit of the Spirit

1. Love: The foundational virtue that motivates and encompasses all other aspects of the fruit of the Spirit. Love is selfless, sacrificial, and unconditional, reflecting the love of Christ.

2. Joy: A deep and abiding sense of happiness and contentment rooted in God's presence and promises, independent of external circumstances.

3. Peace: Inner tranquility and harmony with God and others, resulting from reconciliation through Christ.

4. Patience: The ability to endure difficult circumstances and people with a calm and forgiving spirit, reflecting God's patience with us.

5. Kindness: A disposition to be gentle, compassionate, and helpful toward others, motivated by genuine care and concern.

6. Goodness: Moral integrity and a desire to do what is right, demonstrating God's character in our actions.

7. Faithfulness: Loyalty and reliability in our relationships with God and others, grounded in trustworthiness and commitment.

8. Gentleness: A humble and considerate approach to others, avoiding harshness and aggression.

9. Self-Control: The ability to exercise restraint and discipline over our desires and impulses, aligning our actions with God's will.

The Centrality of Love in the Fruit of the Spirit

Paul lists love first among the fruit of the Spirit, highlighting its central role in the Christian life. Love is the root from which all other virtues grow, and it is the primary evidence of the Spirit's work within us.

1. Love as the Foundation:

- Motivating Virtue: Love motivates the development of other virtues. For example, joy and peace flow from a heart filled with love for God and others.

- Integrating Virtue: Love integrates and holds together all aspects of the fruit of the Spirit. Without love, other virtues lose their coherence and effectiveness.

2. Love and Community:

- Building Relationships: Love is essential for healthy, Christ-centered relationships. It fosters unity, trust, and mutual support within the body of Christ.

- Serving Others: Love drives believers to serve others selflessly, reflecting the example of Jesus and fulfilling the law's true intent.

3. Love and Witness:

- Reflecting Christ: A life marked by love bears witness to the transformative power of the gospel. Jesus said, "By this everyone will know that you are my disciples, if you love one another" (John 13:35).

- Drawing Others to Christ: Love attracts others to the faith, demonstrating the reality of God's love and the difference it makes in our lives.

Living by the Spirit

Paul exhorts believers to live by the Spirit, allowing the Holy Spirit to guide and empower their daily lives. This involves a continuous process of yielding to the Spirit's influence and rejecting the desires of the flesh.

Walking in the Spirit

1. Daily Surrender:

- Prayer and Dependence: Regular prayer and dependence on the Holy Spirit are crucial for walking in the Spirit. This involves asking for His guidance, strength, and wisdom in all aspects of life.

- Scripture and Meditation: Immersing ourselves in God's Word and meditating on its truths helps align our hearts and minds with the Spirit's leading.

2. Active Participation:

- Obedience and Action: Walking in the Spirit requires active participation in God's work. This means obeying His commands, engaging in acts of service, and bearing witness to His love.

- Community and Accountability: Being part of a Christian community provides support, encouragement, and accountability in our spiritual journey. Together, we can help each other live by the Spirit.

Overcoming the Flesh

1. Recognizing Temptations:

- Awareness and Vigilance: Being aware of our weaknesses and the temptations we face is the first step in overcoming the flesh. Vigilance in prayer and self-examination helps us stay alert.

- Resisting Sin: Actively resisting sin involves fleeing from temptation, seeking God's help, and relying on the strength of the Spirit.

2. Embracing Transformation:

- Renewing the Mind: Allowing the Holy Spirit to renew our minds transforms our thoughts and attitudes, making us more like Christ (Romans 12:2).

- Cultivating Virtues: Intentionally cultivating the fruit of the Spirit in our lives leads to the gradual transformation of our character.

Conclusion

Paul's contrast between the works of the flesh and the fruit of the Spirit in Galatians 5:19-23 underscores the transformative power of the Holy Spirit in the lives of believers. The works of the flesh lead to spiritual death and relational destruction, while the fruit of the Spirit brings life, peace, and unity.

At the heart of the fruit of the Spirit is love, the foundational virtue that integrates and motivates all other aspects of the Spirit's work within us. Love is central to the Christian life, guiding our relationships, service, and witness.

Living by the Spirit involves a daily surrender to His guidance, active participation in God's work, and continuous transformation of our hearts and minds. By embracing the fruit of the Spirit, believers can overcome the flesh and live lives that reflect the character of Christ.

As we strive to walk in the Spirit and cultivate the fruit of love, we fulfill the law's true intent and bear witness to the world of the transformative power of God's love. In this way, Paul's teaching becomes a practical and powerful guide for Christian living, shaping individuals and communities according to God's perfect will.

CHAPTER 04

LOVE IN THE BODY OF CHRIST

Ephesians 4:1-16: Unity and Maturity in Love

In his letter to the Ephesians, Apostle Paul provides a detailed exposition on the unity and maturity of the body of Christ, emphasizing the critical role of love. Ephesians 4:1-16 outlines how believers are to live in a manner worthy of their calling, maintaining the bond of peace through love and growing into maturity as one body. This chapter explores the importance of unity in the Spirit and how love serves as the foundation for maintaining peace and fostering growth within the church.

The Call to Unity

Paul begins Ephesians 4 with a passionate plea for unity among believers. He urges them to live in a manner worthy of their calling, characterized by humility, gentleness, patience, and love.

Living Worthy of the Calling

1. Humility and Gentleness:

- Humility: Recognizing our dependence on God and valuing others above ourselves. Humility involves a lowliness of mind that seeks to honor others.

- Gentleness: A kind and considerate approach to others, avoiding harshness and aggression. Gentleness reflects Christ's meekness and is essential for maintaining unity.

2. Patience and Forbearance:

- Patience: The ability to endure difficult circumstances and people with a calm and forgiving spirit. Patience is crucial for fostering lasting relationships.

- Bearing with One Another in Love: Love is the foundation for enduring each other's faults and imperfections. It involves a commitment to the well-being of others, even when it is challenging.

3. Eager to Maintain Unity:

- The Bond of Peace: Paul calls believers to be eager to maintain the unity of the Spirit in the bond of peace. This unity is a gift of the Spirit, and believers are responsible for preserving it through their actions and attitudes.

The Basis of Unity

Paul grounds the call for unity in the fundamental truths of the Christian faith. He outlines the basis of unity in a series of seven affirmations, each emphasizing the oneness of the body of Christ.

Seven Affirmations of Unity

1. One Body:

- The Church: There is one body, the universal church, composed of all believers in Christ. This body transcends denominational and cultural boundaries, united by faith in Jesus.

2. One Spirit:

- The Holy Spirit: The same Holy Spirit indwells all believers, empowering and guiding them. The Spirit's presence is the source of unity within the church.

3. One Hope:

- The Hope of Salvation: Believers share one hope, the assurance of eternal life and the fulfillment of God's promises. This hope unites believers in their journey toward the ultimate realization of God's kingdom.

4. One Lord:

- Jesus Christ: There is one Lord, Jesus Christ, who is the head of the church. Believers are united under His lordship, acknowledging Him as their Savior and King.

5. One Faith:

- The Christian Faith: Believers share one faith, the core doctrines of Christianity that define their belief in the gospel. This common faith provides a foundation for unity.

6. One Baptism:

- Baptism into Christ: There is one baptism, symbolizing believers' identification with Christ in His death, burial, and resurrection. Baptism is a sign of the new covenant and entry into the body of Christ.

7. One God and Father:

- God the Father: There is one God and Father of all, who is over all and through all and in all. The universal fatherhood of God unites all believers as His children.

The Role of Love in Unity

Love is central to maintaining the unity of the Spirit and the bond of peace. It is the driving force behind the attitudes and actions that preserve unity within the church.

Love as the Bond of Peace

1. Selfless Love:

- Putting Others First: Love involves putting others' needs and well-being above our own. It means seeking the good of others and being willing to make sacrifices for their benefit.

- Serving in Love: Selfless love manifests in acts of service and kindness. Serving one another in love strengthens relationships and fosters a sense of community.

2. Forgiving Love:

- Forgiving Offenses: Love enables believers to forgive one another, just as God in Christ has forgiven them (Ephesians 4:32). Forgiveness is essential for resolving conflicts and maintaining peace.

- Bearing Burdens: Love involves bearing each other's burdens and supporting one another through difficult times (Galatians 6:2). This mutual care and support enhance unity.

3. Patient Love:

- Enduring Patience: Love is patient and enduring, allowing believers to bear with one another's weaknesses and faults. This patience prevents division and promotes harmony.

- Encouraging Growth: Patient love encourages growth and maturity in others. It provides a nurturing environment where individuals can develop and flourish.

Growing into Maturity

Paul emphasizes that unity in the body of Christ leads to spiritual maturity. The church grows into maturity as each member contributes to the well-being and development of the whole.

The Gifts of Christ

1. Diversity of Gifts:

- Variety of Roles: Christ has given diverse gifts to the church, including apostles, prophets, evangelists, pastors, and teachers (Ephesians 4:11). These roles serve different functions but work together for the common good.

- Equipping the Saints: The purpose of these gifts is to equip the saints for the work of ministry, building up the body of Christ (Ephesians 4:12). Equipping involves teaching, training, and empowering believers to serve.

2. Unity in Diversity:

- Complementary Roles: The diversity of gifts and roles reflects the multifaceted nature of the church. Each member has a unique contribution, and together they form a unified and effective body.

- Mutual Dependence: Unity in diversity means that each member depends on the others. This interdependence fosters a sense of belonging and shared purpose.

The Goal of Maturity

1. Attaining the Fullness of Christ:

- Growing in Christlikeness: The ultimate goal is for the church to attain the fullness of Christ, growing into His likeness (Ephesians 4:13). This involves spiritual maturity, moral integrity, and Christlike character.

- Reflecting Christ: As the church grows in maturity, it reflects Christ more fully to the world, bearing witness to His transforming power.

2. Stability and Discernment:

- Sound Doctrine: Maturity involves stability in sound doctrine, preventing believers from being tossed about by false teachings and deceitful schemes (Ephesians 4:14).

- Discernment: Growing in maturity enhances believers' ability to discern truth from error and to stand firm in their faith.

3. Speaking the Truth in Love:

- Truth and Love: Maturity involves speaking the truth in love, balancing honesty with compassion (Ephesians 4:15). This approach promotes healthy relationships and constructive growth.

- Building Up the Body: Speaking the truth in love builds up the body of Christ, fostering an environment where members can thrive and grow.

Conclusion

Paul's teaching in Ephesians 4:1-16 provides a comprehensive framework for understanding the role of love in the unity and maturity of the body of Christ. Unity in the

Spirit is maintained through the bond of peace, which is founded on love. Love is the driving force behind the attitudes and actions that preserve unity and promote harmony within the church.

As believers live in humility, gentleness, patience, and love, they maintain the unity of the Spirit and the bond of peace. This unity is grounded in the fundamental truths of the Christian faith, reflected in the seven affirmations of oneness.

Love also plays a crucial role in fostering spiritual maturity. The diversity of gifts within the church contributes to the growth and development of the whole body. As each member serves in love, the church grows into the fullness of Christ, reflecting His character and bearing witness to His transforming power.

By embracing the principles outlined by Paul, believers can cultivate a community marked by unity and maturity in love. This community serves as a powerful testimony to the world of the reality of God's love and the transforming power of the gospel. In this way, Paul's teaching becomes a practical and powerful guide for Christian living, shaping individuals and communities according to God's perfect will.

Growth in Love: How Love Leads to Spiritual Maturity and the Edification of the Church

In his letter to the Ephesians, Apostle Paul emphasizes the pivotal role of love in the growth and maturity of the church. Ephesians 4:1-16 presents a blueprint for how love fosters spiritual maturity and edifies the body of Christ. This chapter explores how love leads to spiritual growth, strengthens the church, and equips believers to fulfill their calling in Christ.

The Role of Love in Spiritual Maturity

Love is the cornerstone of spiritual maturity. It is through love that believers grow in their relationship with God and with one another, developing Christlike character and contributing to the overall health and unity of the church.

Love as the Foundation of Growth

1. Love for God:

- Deepening Relationship: Love for God is the starting point of spiritual growth. As believers grow in their love for God, they develop a deeper relationship with Him, characterized by worship, obedience, and intimacy.

- Transformative Power: This love transforms believers from the inside out, aligning their desires and actions with God's will. Jesus emphasized the greatest commandment as loving God with all one's heart, soul, and mind (Matthew 22:37).

2. Love for Others:

- Reflecting God's Love: Love for others is a natural outflow of love for God. It reflects God's love in practical ways, through acts of kindness, service, and compassion.

- Fostering Community: This love fosters a sense of community and belonging within the church, where each member is valued and cared for.

Love and the Fruit of the Spirit

Paul lists love as the first attribute of the fruit of the Spirit (Galatians 5:22-23). The presence of the Holy Spirit in a believer's life produces love, which in turn nurtures other spiritual fruits such as joy, peace, patience, kindness, goodness, faithfulness, gentleness, and self-control. These attributes contribute to spiritual maturity and harmonious relationships within the church.

The Dynamics of Love in the Church

Love plays a crucial role in how the church functions and grows together. It influences every aspect of communal life, from leadership and service to conflict resolution and mutual edification.

Leadership in Love

1. Servant Leadership:

- Leading by Example: Church leaders are called to lead by example, demonstrating love in their actions and decisions. Jesus modeled servant leadership by washing His disciples' feet and ultimately sacrificing His life for them (John 13:1-17).

- Shepherding the Flock: Leaders are shepherds who care for the spiritual well-being of their congregation, guiding them with love and wisdom.

2. Equipping the Saints:

- Teaching and Training: Leaders equip the saints for the work of ministry, helping them grow in their faith and use their spiritual gifts effectively (Ephesians 4:11-12).

- Empowering Service: By empowering others to serve, leaders foster a culture of mutual edification and active participation in the life of the church.

Service in Love

1. Using Spiritual Gifts:

- Diverse Gifts: The Holy Spirit distributes a variety of gifts to believers for the common good (1 Corinthians 12:4-7). These gifts include teaching, prophecy, healing, administration, and more.

- Serving in Love: Spiritual gifts are to be exercised in love, with the goal of building up the body of Christ. Love ensures that these gifts are used selflessly and effectively.

2. Acts of Kindness:

- Practical Help: Serving one another in practical ways, such as providing for physical needs, offering support during difficult times, and showing hospitality, strengthens the bonds within the church.

- Encouragement: Acts of encouragement, such as speaking words of affirmation and offering a listening ear, uplift and motivate fellow believers.

Conflict Resolution in Love

1. Seeking Reconciliation:

- Forgiveness: Love involves forgiving others as God has forgiven us. Forgiveness is essential for resolving conflicts and restoring relationships (Ephesians 4:32).

- Pursuing Peace: Believers are called to pursue peace and reconciliation, addressing conflicts directly and with a spirit of humility and love (Matthew 18:15-17).

2. Maintaining Unity:

- Eager to Maintain Unity: Paul urges believers to be eager to maintain the unity of the Spirit in the bond of peace (Ephesians 4:3). This unity is preserved through love and mutual respect.

- Building Bridges: Love builds bridges between individuals and groups within the church, overcoming divisions and fostering a sense of togetherness.

Mutual Edification in Love

1. Speaking the Truth in Love:

- Balancing Truth and Compassion: Speaking the truth in love involves balancing honesty with compassion. This approach promotes growth and avoids unnecessary hurt (Ephesians 4:15).

- Constructive Feedback: Providing constructive feedback helps others grow in their faith and character, contributing to the overall maturity of the church.

2. Supporting Spiritual Growth:

- Discipleship: Investing in discipleship relationships, where more mature believers mentor others, fosters spiritual growth and maturity.

- Prayer and Support: Praying for one another and offering spiritual support strengthens the faith and resilience of fellow believers.

The Outcome of Growth in Love

As the church grows in love, it matures and is built up in unity and strength. This growth is evident in the character of individual believers and the collective health of the church.

Individual Maturity

1. Christlike Character:

- Reflecting Jesus: Mature believers reflect the character of Christ in their daily lives. They exhibit the fruit of the Spirit and live out the principles of love and holiness.

- Continual Growth: Spiritual maturity is an ongoing process. Mature believers continue to seek God's presence, grow in their understanding of His Word, and apply it to their lives.

2. Effective Ministry:

- Using Gifts Wisely: Mature believers use their spiritual gifts effectively, contributing to the church's mission and ministry.

- Serving Faithfully: They serve faithfully, motivated by love for God and others, and are reliable and trustworthy in their commitments.

Corporate Edification

1. Unity and Harmony:

- Unified Body: A church that grows in love and experiences unity and harmony. Members work together, support one another, and share a common purpose in Christ.

- Peace and Stability: This unity creates an environment of peace and stability, where conflicts are resolved quickly, and relationships are strengthened.

2. Effective Witness:

- Demonstrating the Gospel: A loving and mature church effectively demonstrates the gospel to the world. It becomes a beacon of hope, compassion, and truth.

- Attracting Others: The love and unity within the church attract others to the faith. People are drawn to the authenticity and warmth of a community that lives out its beliefs.

Conclusion

Paul's teaching in Ephesians 4:1-16 underscores the critical role of love in the growth and maturity of the church. Love is the foundation upon which spiritual maturity is built and the driving force behind the edification of the body of Christ.

As believers grow in their love for God and for one another, they develop Christlike character and contribute to the overall health and unity of the church. Love influences leadership, service, conflict resolution, and mutual edification, ensuring that the church grows together in harmony and strength.

The outcome of growth in love is a mature and unified church that reflects the character of Christ and effectively witnesses to the world. By embracing Paul's teaching and prioritizing love, believers can cultivate a community that honors God and fulfills His purposes.

In this way, love leads to spiritual maturity and the edification of the church, shaping individuals and communities according to God's perfect will and advancing His kingdom on earth.

Roles within the Church: The Function of Apostles, Prophets, Evangelists, Pastors, and Teachers in Fostering a Community of Love

In Ephesians 4:11-16, Apostle Paul outlines the roles of apostles, prophets, evangelists, pastors, and teachers within the church. These roles are vital for equipping believers, fostering a community of love, and building up the body of Christ. This chapter explores the specific functions of each role and how they contribute to the spiritual growth, unity, and maturity of the church, emphasizing the centrality of love in all these functions.

The Fivefold Ministry

Paul identifies five key roles in the church that are essential for its health and growth. Each role has a unique function but works together in harmony to foster a loving and mature Christian community.

1. Apostles

Role and Function:

- Foundational Leadership: Apostles are foundational leaders who establish and oversee new churches. They are often pioneers, sent out to start new ministries and spread the gospel in unreached areas.

- Vision and Direction: Apostles provide vision and direction for the church, ensuring that its mission aligns with God's purposes. They help to establish core doctrines and practices.

Contribution to Community of Love:

- Unity and Collaboration: Apostles promote unity and collaboration among different churches and ministries, fostering a sense of collective identity and purpose.

- Encouraging Growth: By establishing new communities and nurturing them, apostles help believers grow in their faith and love for one another.

2. Prophets

Role and Function:

- Revelation and Guidance: Prophets receive and communicate God's messages to the church. They provide spiritual insight, warning, and encouragement, helping the church stay aligned with God's will.

- Intercessory Role: Prophets often engage in deep intercessory prayer, standing in the gap for the church and seeking God's direction.

Contribution to Community of Love:

- Encouragement and Edification: Prophets build up the church by encouraging and edifying believers, strengthening their faith and love.

- Corrective Love: Prophets call the church to repentance and renewal, addressing areas of sin and disobedience with love and compassion.

3. Evangelists

Role and Function:

- Spreading the Gospel: Evangelists are dedicated to preaching the gospel and bringing people to faith in Christ. They often work outside the church, reaching out to the lost.

- Training and Mobilizing: Evangelists train and mobilize other believers to share their faith, equipping the church for evangelistic outreach.

Contribution to Community of Love:

- Welcoming New Believers: Evangelists help integrate new believers into the church community, ensuring they feel welcomed and loved.

- Inspiring Passion: Their passion for the gospel inspires the church to love the lost and engage in mission, extending the reach of the church's love.

4. Pastors

Role and Function:

- Shepherding the Flock: Pastors provide pastoral care, nurturing and guiding the spiritual growth of the congregation. They are often involved in counseling, comforting, and supporting members.

- Teaching and Preaching: Pastors regularly teach and preach God's Word, providing biblical instruction and encouragement.

Contribution to Community of Love:

- Personal Care: Pastors foster a loving community by providing personal care and attention to individuals, helping them feel valued and supported.

- Building Relationships: They create a sense of family within the church, encouraging strong, loving relationships among members.

5. Teachers

Role and Function:

- Biblical Instruction: Teachers are responsible for providing sound biblical teaching, helping believers understand and apply God's Word to their lives.

- Discipleship: Teachers often lead discipleship programs, Bible studies, and educational initiatives within the church.

Contribution to Community of Love:

- Spiritual Growth: By deepening believers' understanding of Scripture, teachers foster spiritual growth and maturity, helping them love God and others more fully.

- Unity in Truth: Sound teaching promotes unity in the church by grounding believers in shared truths and values.

Equipping the Saints

The primary purpose of these five roles is to equip the saints for the work of ministry and to build up the body of Christ (Ephesians 4:12). This equipping involves teaching, training, mentoring, and empowering believers to use their gifts and serve one another in love.

Building Up the Body

1. Developing Gifts:

- Identifying and Nurturing: Leaders help believers identify their spiritual gifts and provide opportunities for them to develop and use these gifts in service to the church and community.

- Mentorship: Experienced leaders mentor emerging leaders, fostering a culture of growth and multiplication within the church.

2. Promoting Active Participation:

- Encouraging Involvement: Leaders encourage all members to actively participate in the life of the church, emphasizing that every person has a role to play in building up the body.

- Creating Opportunities: By creating opportunities for service and ministry, leaders help believers engage in meaningful and impactful work that benefits the community.

Strengthening Unity and Maturity

1. Fostering Unity:

- Shared Vision: Leaders promote a shared vision and mission, uniting the church around common goals and values.

- Conflict Resolution: They help resolve conflicts and promote reconciliation, ensuring that love and unity are maintained within the church.

2. Encouraging Maturity:

- Spiritual Growth: Through teaching, discipleship, and example, leaders encourage believers to grow in their faith, character, and love for God and others.

- Holistic Development: Leaders focus on the holistic development of believers, addressing their spiritual, emotional, relational, and practical needs.

The Centrality of Love

Love is the glue that holds the body of Christ together. It is the underlying principle that guides the actions and attitudes of apostles, prophets, evangelists, pastors, and teachers. Without love, their work would be ineffective and meaningless.

Love as the Motivation

1. Selfless Service:

- Serving Others: Love motivates leaders to serve others selflessly, putting the needs of the congregation above their own.

- Sacrificial Giving: True love involves sacrificial giving, whether of time, resources, or energy, to benefit others.

2. Genuine Care:

- Compassion and Empathy: Leaders are called to genuinely care for their flock, showing compassion and empathy in their interactions.

- Building Relationships: Love fosters strong, authentic relationships within the church, creating a supportive and nurturing environment.

Love as the Goal

1. Edification:

- Building Up: The ultimate goal of the fivefold ministry is to build up the body of Christ in love. This involves strengthening faith, deepening relationships, and promoting spiritual growth.

- Encouraging and Exhorting: Leaders encourage and exhort believers to live out their faith in love, helping them grow into maturity.

2. Unity and Harmony:

- Promoting Peace: Love promotes peace and harmony within the church, ensuring that differences are handled with grace and understanding.

- Fostering Inclusion: A loving church is inclusive, welcoming all people and valuing each person's unique contribution.

Conclusion

Paul's teaching in Ephesians 4:11-16 highlights the importance of the roles of apostles, prophets, evangelists, pastors, and teachers in fostering a community of love. Each role has a unique function but works together to equip the saints, build up the body of Christ, and promote unity and maturity.

The centrality of love in these roles cannot be overstated. Love motivates leaders to serve selflessly, care genuinely, and build up the church in unity and harmony. As believers grow in love, they develop Christlike character and contribute to the overall health and strength of the church.

By embracing their roles and working together in love, apostles, prophets, evangelists, pastors, and teachers can create a thriving, loving community that reflects the heart of Christ and advances His kingdom on earth. This community serves as a powerful testimony to the world of the transformative power of God's love and the reality of the gospel.

In this way, Paul's teaching becomes a practical and powerful guide for Christian living, shaping individuals and communities according to God's perfect will and fostering a church that is united, mature, and rooted in love.

CHAPTER 05

LOVE AND SACRIFICE

Philippians 2:1-11: The Example of Christ

In Philippians 2:1-11, Apostle Paul presents one of the most profound and inspiring passages in the New Testament, emphasizing the importance of humility and self-sacrifice in the Christian life. This passage, often referred to as the "Christ Hymn," provides a powerful example of love and sacrifice through the life and actions of Jesus Christ. This chapter explores the mind of Christ, encouraging believers to emulate His humility and self-sacrifice as the ultimate expression of love.

The Mind of Christ

Paul begins this section by calling the Philippians to adopt the same mindset as Christ Jesus. This mindset is characterized by humility, selflessness, and a willingness to serve others, even at great personal cost.

Unity and Humility

1. Unity through Humility:

- Encouragement in Christ: Paul appeals to the encouragement believers find in their relationship with Christ, urging them to be united in spirit and purpose (Philippians 2:1).

- Comfort from Love: The comfort and love believers receive from Christ should motivate them to show the same love to one another, fostering unity (Philippians 2:2).

2. Selflessness and Consideration:

- Do Nothing Out of Selfish Ambition: Paul exhorts believers to reject selfish ambition and vain conceit, instead embracing humility and considering others more significant than themselves (Philippians 2:3).

- Looking to Others' Interests: True humility involves looking not only to one's own interests but also to the interests of others, prioritizing their well-being (Philippians 2:4).

The Example of Christ

To illustrate this mindset, Paul points to the ultimate example of humility and self-sacrifice: Jesus Christ. He describes Christ's journey from divine glory to human servanthood, culminating in His sacrificial death on the cross.

1. Christ's Humiliation:

- Equality with God: Jesus, being in the very nature of God, did not consider equality with God something to be exploited for His own advantage (Philippians 2:6). This highlights His preexistence and divine nature.

- Emptied Himself: Instead, He emptied Himself, taking on the form of a servant and being made in human likeness (Philippians 2:7). This "kenosis," or self-emptying, is a profound act of humility, as the Creator became part of His creation.

2. Christ's Servanthood:

- Human Likeness: Jesus fully embraced human nature, experiencing the limitations and challenges of human life (Philippians 2:7).

- Obedient to Death: He humbled Himself further by becoming obedient to death, even death on a cross (Philippians 2:8). This sacrificial obedience exemplifies the depth of His love and commitment to humanity's redemption.

3. Christ's Exaltation:

- Exalted by God: Because of His humility and obedience, God exalted Jesus to the highest place and gave Him the name that is above every name (Philippians 2:9). This exaltation vindicates His sacrifice and affirms His lordship.

- Every Knee Shall Bow: At the name of Jesus, every knee shall bow, in heaven and on earth and under the earth, and every tongue confess that Jesus Christ is Lord, to the glory of God the Father (Philippians 2:10-11). This universal acknowledgment underscores His ultimate authority and the glory of His sacrificial love.

Emulating Christ's Humility and Self-Sacrifice

Paul's call to emulate the mind of Christ is not just an ideal but a practical guide for Christian living. By following Christ's example of humility and self-sacrifice, believers can embody His love in their daily lives and relationships.

Practical Steps to Emulate Christ

1. Cultivating Humility:

   - Recognize Our Dependence on God: Humility begins with acknowledging our dependence on God for everything. This recognition fosters a spirit of gratitude and reverence.

   - Serve Others Selflessly: True humility involves serving others without seeking recognition or reward. By putting others' needs above our own, we reflect Christ's servant heart.

2. Embracing Self-Sacrifice:

   - Willingness to Suffer for Others: Following Christ's example means being willing to endure hardship and make sacrifices for the benefit of others. This might involve giving up time, resources, or personal comfort.

   - Obedience to God's Will: Like Christ, we are called to be obedient to God's will, even when it is difficult. This obedience is an expression of our love for God and our trust in His purposes.

3. Promoting Unity:

- Fostering a Spirit of Cooperation: Humility and self-sacrifice promote unity within the church. By considering others' interests and working together harmoniously, we build a strong, loving community.

- Resolving Conflicts Peacefully: Emulating Christ's humility helps us approach conflicts with a spirit of reconciliation and peace, seeking to restore relationships rather than asserting our own way.

The Transformative Power of Christ's Example

1. Personal Transformation:

- Character Development: Emulating Christ's humility and self-sacrifice leads to personal growth and character development. We become more patient, compassionate, and resilient.

- Spiritual Maturity: Following Christ's example deepens our spiritual maturity, strengthening our relationship with God and our understanding of His will.

2. Community Transformation:

- Building a Loving Church: A church that embraces humility and self-sacrifice is marked by love, unity, and mutual support. This community reflects the heart of Christ and attracts others to the faith.

- Impact on the World: The example of a loving, sacrificial community has a powerful impact on the world. It demonstrates the reality of the gospel and offers hope to those seeking meaning and connection.

Conclusion

Paul's teaching in Philippians 2:1-11 presents a powerful and challenging example of love and sacrifice through the life of Jesus Christ. Emulating the mind of Christ involves cultivating humility, embracing self-sacrifice, and promoting unity within the church. By following Christ's example, believers can embody His love in their daily lives and relationships, fostering a community that reflects His heart and advances His kingdom.

The transformative power of Christ's humility and self-sacrifice extends beyond individual lives to impact the entire church and the world. As believers grow in their understanding and practice of these virtues, they contribute to the spiritual maturity and edification of the church, creating a loving and unified community that bears witness to the gospel.

In this way, Paul's teaching becomes a practical and powerful guide for Christian living, shaping individuals and communities according to God's perfect will and demonstrating the depth and beauty of Christ's love and sacrifice.

Love as Sacrificial Service: Practical Examples of Living Out Sacrificial Love

In the New Testament, the concept of love is intricately linked with sacrifice. Jesus Christ's life and ministry exemplified sacrificial love, setting a standard for believers to follow. Sacrificial love involves putting others' needs above our own, serving selflessly, and making personal sacrifices for the benefit of others. This chapter explores practical examples of living out sacrificial love, drawing from biblical teachings and real-life applications.

The Biblical Basis for Sacrificial Love

Sacrificial love is a central theme in the teachings of Jesus and the apostles. The New Testament provides numerous examples and instructions on how believers can embody this type of love in their daily lives.

Jesus is the Ultimate Example

1. The Sacrifice of the Cross:

   - Atoning Sacrifice: Jesus' death on the cross is the ultimate demonstration of sacrificial love. He gave His life to atone for the sins of humanity, offering Himself as a ransom for many (Mark 10:45).

- Selfless Love: Jesus' willingness to endure suffering and death for the sake of others exemplifies the depth of His love and sets a standard for believers to follow.

2. Servant Leadership:

- Washing the Disciples' Feet: In John 13, Jesus washes His disciples' feet, an act of humility and service. He instructs His followers to do likewise, serving one another in love (John 13:14-15).

- Teaching on Service: Jesus taught that greatness in His kingdom is measured by one's willingness to serve others (Matthew 20:26-28).

The Apostolic Teachings

1. Paul's Exhortations:

- Living Sacrifices: Paul urges believers to present their bodies as living sacrifices, holy and pleasing to God (Romans 12:1). This involves dedicating every aspect of our lives to God's service.

- Bearing One Another's Burdens: In Galatians 6:2, Paul instructs believers to bear one another's burdens, fulfilling the law of Christ. This calls for practical acts of support and care.

2. John's Emphasis on Love:

- Laying Down Our Lives: John writes that we should love not just in words but in actions and that we ought to lay down our lives for our brothers and sisters (1 John 3:16-18).

- Imitating Christ's Love: John emphasizes that believers should love one another as Christ has loved us, which involves self-sacrifice and service (John 15:12-13).

Practical Examples of Sacrificial Love

Living out sacrificial love involves practical actions that reflect the selfless and servant-hearted nature of Christ. These examples provide tangible ways believers can embody this love in various contexts.

In the Family

1. Spousal Relationships:

- Mutual Submission: Husbands and wives are called to submit to one another out of reverence for Christ (Ephesians 5:21). This involves putting each other's needs and well-being first.

- Sacrificial Love: Husbands are instructed to love their wives as Christ loved the church, giving themselves up for them (Ephesians 5:25). This includes making personal sacrifices to support and care for their spouse.

2. Parenting:

- Selfless Parenting: Parents are to raise their children with love and care, often putting their children's needs above their own. This involves sacrifices of time, energy, and resources.

- Teaching and Guiding: Parents sacrifice their own comfort to guide and teach their children in the ways of the Lord, investing in their spiritual and moral development.

In the Church

1. Serving in Ministry:

- Volunteering Time: Church members can volunteer their time and talents to serve in various ministries, such as teaching, hospitality, music, and outreach programs.

- Supporting Others: Providing support to those in need within the church community, whether through financial help, emotional support, or practical assistance, reflects sacrificial love.

2. Community Care:

- Visiting the Sick and Elderly: Visiting and caring for the sick, elderly, and shut-ins demonstrates Christ's love in action. This might involve providing meals, running errands, or simply offering companionship.

- Helping the Needy: Organizing and participating in food drives, clothing donations, and other charitable activities to support those in need within the community.

In the Workplace

1. Ethical Conduct:

- Integrity and Honesty: Maintaining integrity and honesty in business dealings, even when it might be disadvantageous, reflects a commitment to Christlike behavior.

- Serving Others: Using one's position to serve colleagues and clients with kindness and respect, prioritizing their needs and well-being over personal gain.

2. Supporting Colleagues:

- Mentorship: Offering time and expertise to mentor and support less experienced colleagues, helping them grow professionally and personally.

- Teamwork: Being willing to take on additional tasks or cover for colleagues when needed, demonstrating a team-oriented and selfless attitude.

In the Community

1. Acts of Kindness:

- Helping Neighbors: Providing practical help to neighbors, such as assisting with household chores, offering rides, or babysitting, reflects Christ's love in everyday interactions.

- Random Acts of Kindness: Performing random acts of kindness, such as paying for someone's meal or leaving encouraging notes, can brighten someone's day and demonstrate sacrificial love.

2. Advocacy and Justice:

- Standing for the Oppressed: Advocating for social justice and standing up for the oppressed and marginalized reflects Christ's concern for justice and compassion.

- Volunteering for Causes: Committing time and resources to volunteer for causes that promote the common good, such as environmental conservation, education, and healthcare.

Overcoming Challenges in Living Out Sacrificial Love

Living out sacrificial love is not without its challenges. However, by relying on God's strength and guidance, believers can overcome these obstacles and remain faithful to their calling.

Dealing with Self-Centeredness

1. Cultivating a Servant Heart:

- Daily Surrender: Surrendering daily to God's will helps cultivate a servant heart, willing to serve others selflessly.

- Practicing Gratitude: Regularly practicing gratitude for God's blessings helps shift focus from self to others, fostering a spirit of generosity.

2. Seeking Accountability:

- Accountability Partners: Seeking accountability from fellow believers provides support and encouragement in maintaining a selfless attitude.

- Regular Reflection: Regularly reflecting on Christ's example of sacrificial love helps keep the focus on serving others.

Addressing Burnout

1. Finding Balance:

- Setting Boundaries: Setting healthy boundaries ensures that believers do not overextend themselves, leading to burnout. It is important to balance service with rest and self-care.

- Delegating Responsibilities: Sharing responsibilities within the community helps prevent burnout and ensures that the burden of service is distributed.

2. Seeking Renewal:

- Spiritual Renewal: Regular times of prayer, worship, and reflection renew the spirit and provide strength for continued service. Connecting with God is essential for sustaining a heart of service.

- Community Support: Receiving support from the community, whether through encouragement, prayer, or practical help, renews and strengthens those serving.

Conclusion

Sacrificial love is at the heart of the Christian faith, exemplified by Jesus Christ's life, ministry, and ultimate sacrifice on the cross. Paul's teachings, along with those of other apostles, call believers to live out this love in practical, tangible ways in their daily lives.

By embracing humility, selflessness, and a willingness to serve others, believers can embody Christ's sacrificial love in their families, churches, workplaces, and communities. These acts of sacrificial love not only fulfill God's commandments but also bear powerful witness to the transformative power of the gospel.

Living out sacrificial love involves overcoming challenges such as self-centeredness and burnout, but with God's help and the support of the Christian community, believers can remain faithful to their calling. In doing so, they contribute to the growth, unity, and maturity of the body of Christ, reflecting the love and sacrifice of their Savior.

As believers continue to follow Christ's example, they can create a ripple effect of love and service that extends beyond their immediate circles, impacting the world and advancing God's kingdom on earth. In this way, sacrificial love becomes a practical and powerful guide for Christian living, shaping individuals and communities according to God's perfect will.

The Kenosis Hymn: Understanding Christ's Incarnation and Sacrifice as the Ultimate Demonstration of Love

In Philippians 2:5-11, Apostle Paul presents a powerful passage known as the Kenosis Hymn, which profoundly encapsulates the humility, incarnation, and sacrificial love of Jesus Christ. The term "kenosis" comes from the Greek word for "emptying," and this hymn describes how Christ emptied Himself of divine privileges to become a servant and ultimately sacrifice Himself for humanity. This chapter delves into the theological depth of the Kenosis Hymn, exploring Christ's incarnation and sacrifice as the ultimate demonstration of love, and its implications for believers today.

The Kenosis Hymn: Philippians 2:5-11

The Kenosis Hymn is one of the most theologically rich passages in the New Testament, offering deep insights into the nature and mission of Jesus Christ. Paul uses this hymn to illustrate the mind of Christ and to call believers to emulate His humility and sacrificial love.

The Mind of Christ

1. Exhortation to Imitate Christ:

- Verse 5: "In your relationships with one another, have the same mindset as Christ Jesus."

- Paul urges believers to adopt the mindset of Christ, characterized by humility, selflessness, and love.

2. Christ's Preexistence and Equality with God:

- Verse 6: "Who, being in very nature God, did not consider equality with God something to be used to his own advantage."

- Jesus, being fully divine, did not cling to His divine privileges or status. His equality with God was not something He exploited for personal gain.

Christ's Incarnation and Humiliation

1. The Self-Emptying (Kenosis):

- Verse 7: "Rather, he made himself nothing by taking the very nature of a servant, being made in human likeness."

- Christ emptied Himself (kenosis) by taking on human nature. This self-emptying involved renouncing the privileges of His divine status and embracing the limitations of humanity.

2. The Form of a Servant:

- Verse 7: "Taking the very nature of a servant, being made in human likeness."

- Jesus did not just become human; He became a servant. His life was marked by humility and service to others, embodying the servant-hearted nature of God.

Christ's Obedience and Sacrifice

1. Obedience to Death:

- Verse 8: "And being found in appearance as a man, he humbled himself by becoming obedient to death—even death on a cross!"

- Jesus' obedience extended to the point of death. His sacrificial death on the cross was the ultimate act of obedience and love, bearing the sins of humanity.

2. The Ultimate Sacrifice:

- The cross was a symbol of shame and suffering, yet Christ endured it out of love for humanity. His sacrificial death reconciled humanity with God, offering forgiveness and redemption.

Christ's Exaltation

1. God's Response to Christ's Humility:

- Verse 9: "Therefore God exalted him to the highest place and gave him the name that is above every name."

- Because of His humility and obedience, God exalted Jesus, bestowing upon Him the highest honor and authority.

2. Universal Acknowledgment of Christ's Lordship:

- Verses 10-11: "That at the name of Jesus, every knee should bow, in heaven and on earth and under the earth, and every tongue acknowledge that Jesus Christ is Lord, to the glory of God the Father."

- Every being will ultimately recognize and confess Jesus as Lord, bringing glory to God the Father. This universal acknowledgment underscores the supremacy of Christ.

Theological Implications of the Kenosis Hymn

The Kenosis Hymn provides profound theological insights into the nature of Christ's incarnation and sacrifice. It reveals the depths of God's love and the lengths to which He went to redeem humanity.

The Humility of Christ

1. Divine Humility:

- The incarnation demonstrates God's willingness to humble Himself for the sake of humanity. Jesus, though fully divine, took on human form and lived a life of humility and service.

2. Model of Humility:

- Christ's humility serves as a model for believers. Paul calls Christians to emulate this humility in their relationships, valuing others above themselves and serving selflessly.

The Sacrificial Love of Christ

1. Self-Emptying Love:

- Christ's kenosis, or self-emptying, is the ultimate expression of sacrificial love. He gave up His divine privileges and embraced the suffering and limitations of human existence.

2. Redemptive Sacrifice:

- Jesus' sacrificial death on the cross is the pinnacle of His love for humanity. His willingness to die for the sins of the world demonstrates the depths of His love and commitment to redeeming humanity.

The Exaltation of Christ

1. Vindication and Glory:

- God's exaltation of Christ is the divine vindication of His humility and obedience. It affirms His lordship and the effectiveness of His sacrificial work.

2. Universal Lordship:

- The recognition of Jesus as Lord by all creation highlights His supreme authority and the fulfillment of God's redemptive plan. It points to the ultimate triumph of God's love and justice.

Practical Implications for Believers

Understanding the Kenosis Hymn has significant practical implications for how believers live out their faith. Emulating Christ's humility and sacrificial love transforms personal conduct, relationships, and community life.

Emulating Christ's Humility

1. Cultivating Humility:

- Daily Surrender: Believers are called to daily surrender their own will and desires to God, embracing humility in their walk with Christ.

- Serving Others: Emulating Christ involves serving others selflessly, putting their needs above our own and seeking ways to help and support them.

2. Practicing Selflessness:

- Considering Others First: Humility means considering others more significant than ourselves and prioritizing their well-being (Philippians 2:3).

- Acts of Kindness: Practical acts of kindness and service reflect Christ's humble heart and build up the body of Christ.

Living Out Sacrificial Love

1. Sacrificial Giving:

- Time and Resources: Sacrificial love involves giving of our time, resources, and energy to support and care for others, even when it requires personal sacrifice.

- Generosity: Being generous with our possessions, offering help to those in need, and supporting the work of the church and missions.

2. Enduring Hardships for Others:

- Bearing Burdens: Sacrificial love means bearing one another's burdens and supporting others through difficult times (Galatians 6:2).

- Suffering for the Gospel: Being willing to endure hardship, persecution, and suffering for the sake of the gospel and the well-being of others.

Fostering Unity and Community

1. Promoting Unity:

- Shared Purpose: Emulating Christ's humility and sacrificial love promotes unity within the church, as believers work together for the common good.

- Resolving Conflicts: Addressing conflicts with a spirit of humility and seeking reconciliation and peace, following Christ's example of love and forgiveness.

2. Building a Loving Community:

- Encouragement and Support: Creating a supportive and encouraging environment where members feel valued and cared for, reflecting the love of Christ.

- Inclusive Love: Welcoming and including everyone in the community, regardless of their background, and showing unconditional love.

Conclusion

The Kenosis Hymn in Philippians 2:5-11 provides a profound and powerful depiction of Christ's incarnation and sacrifice as the ultimate demonstration of love. Jesus' humility, self-emptying, and sacrificial death exemplify the depths of God's love for humanity and set a standard for believers to follow.

Understanding and emulating the mind of Christ has profound theological and practical implications. It calls believers to cultivate humility, live out sacrificial love, and foster unity within the church. By following Christ's example, believers can embody His love in their daily lives, transforming their relationships and communities.

As believers grow in their understanding and practice of Christlike humility and sacrificial love, they reflect the heart of Christ and contribute to the growth, unity, and maturity of the body of Christ. This emulation of Christ's love not only fulfills God's commandments but also bears powerful witness to the transformative power of the gospel, advancing God's kingdom on earth.

In this way, the Kenosis Hymn becomes a practical and powerful guide for Christian living, shaping individuals and communities according to God's perfect will and demonstrating the depth and beauty of Christ's love and sacrifice.

CHAPTER 06

LOVE AND SUFFERING

2 Corinthians 12:7-10: Strength in Weakness

In 2 Corinthians 12:7-10, Apostle Paul provides a deeply personal account of his own struggles, revealing how he learned to rely on God's grace amidst suffering. This passage offers profound insights into the relationship between love and suffering, emphasizing the paradoxical strength found in weakness. This chapter explores Paul's "thorn in the flesh," his personal struggles, and how his reliance on God's grace serves as a powerful example for believers facing their own trials.

Paul's Thorn in the Flesh

Paul's "thorn in the flesh" is one of the most discussed and debated aspects of his writings. While the exact nature of this thorn remains unclear, its impact on Paul and his ministry is unmistakable.

The Nature of the Thorn

1. Persistent Affliction:

- Verse 7: "Therefore, in order to keep me from becoming conceited, I was given a thorn in my flesh, a messenger of Satan, to torment me."

- Paul describes the thorn as a persistent affliction that tormented him. This suggests it was a significant and ongoing challenge, causing him considerable distress.

2. Humbling Experience:

- The thorn was given to keep Paul humble and to prevent him from becoming conceited due to the extraordinary revelations he had received. This indicates that, despite his spiritual experiences and accomplishments, Paul was not immune to pride and needed this affliction to maintain his humility.

Paul's Plea for Relief

1. Repeated Requests:

- Verse 8: "Three times I pleaded with the Lord to take it away from me."

- Paul prayed earnestly and repeatedly for God to remove the thorn. His plea for relief highlights his human vulnerability and his desire for the affliction to be lifted.

2. God's Response:

- Verse 9: "But he said to me, 'My grace is sufficient for you, for my power is made perfect in weakness.'"

- Instead of removing the thorn, God provided Paul with a profound answer: His grace was sufficient. This response shifted Paul's perspective from seeking relief to embracing God's sustaining grace.

Strength in Weakness

God's response to Paul's plea reveals a profound truth about the relationship between human weakness and divine strength. Paul's experience teaches believers how to find strength in their own weaknesses through reliance on God's grace.

Embracing Weakness

1. Divine Power in Human Weakness:

- Verse 9: "Therefore I will boast all the more gladly about my weaknesses, so that Christ's power may rest on me."

- Paul learned to boast in his weaknesses because it was in these very weaknesses that Christ's power was most evident. This counterintuitive approach underscores the paradox of strength in weakness.

2. Redefining Success:

- Redefining Strength: In the world's eyes, strength is often associated with power, control, and independence. However, Paul redefines strength as complete reliance on

God. True strength is found in acknowledging our limitations and depending on God's limitless power.

Relying on God's Grace

1. Sufficient Grace:

- God's Assurance: God assured Paul that His grace was sufficient. This sufficiency means that God's grace is enough to sustain, empower, and comfort us in every circumstance.

- Continuous Dependence: Relying on God's grace involves a continuous, daily dependence on Him. It's an acknowledgment that we cannot navigate life's challenges on our own and need His constant support.

2. Perfected Power:

- Verse 9: "For my power is made perfect in weakness."

- God's power is perfected, or brought to its full expression, in human weakness. When believers are weak, God's strength is most clearly seen and experienced. This dynamic allows God to receive the glory, as it becomes evident that the strength comes from Him and not from human effort.

Insights from Paul's Personal Struggles

Paul's experience with his thorn in the flesh offers valuable insights for believers facing their own struggles. It teaches important lessons about humility, reliance on God, and the transformative power of suffering.

Humility Through Suffering

1. Acknowledging Limitations:

- Suffering humbles us by highlighting our limitations and our need for God. It strips away our self-sufficiency and drives us to seek God's help and comfort.

- Paul's Example: Despite his profound spiritual experiences and significant ministry, Paul remained humble, recognizing that his strength came from God, not from his own abilities.

2. Preventing Conceit:

- Paul's thorn in the flesh prevented him from becoming conceited. Similarly, suffering can keep us grounded, preventing pride and keeping us reliant on God.

- Spiritual Growth: Humility fosters spiritual growth, as it creates an environment where God can work more freely in our lives. When we are humble, we are more open to God's guidance and correction.

Reliance on God's Grace

1. Trusting God's Sufficiency:

- Trusting in God's grace means believing that He is enough, even when circumstances are difficult. It involves resting in His promises and relying on His strength rather than our own.

- Daily Dependence: This reliance is not a one-time decision but a daily practice of turning to God for strength, wisdom, and comfort.

2. Finding Peace in God's Presence:

- God's grace provides peace and comfort in the midst of suffering. Knowing that God is with us and that His grace is sufficient helps us endure and find hope even in the darkest times.

- Paul's Peace: Despite his ongoing affliction, Paul found peace and strength in God's presence, allowing him to continue his ministry with confidence and joy.

The Transformative Power of Suffering

1. Developing Resilience:

- Suffering can develop resilience and perseverance. As we face challenges and rely on God's strength, we become stronger in our faith and more resilient in the face of future trials.

- Paul's Endurance: Paul's endurance in suffering is a testament to the power of God's grace. His life demonstrates that suffering can be a catalyst for spiritual growth and greater reliance on God.

2. Bearing Witness to God's Power:

- Our response to suffering can bear powerful witness to God's grace and strength. When others see us enduring hardships with faith and confidence in God, it can inspire and encourage them.

- Paul's Testimony: Paul's testimony of strength in weakness continues to inspire believers today. His life shows that God's power is sufficient to sustain us through any trial.

Conclusion

Paul's teaching in 2 Corinthians 12:7-10 provides profound insights into the relationship between love, suffering, and divine strength. His experience with the thorn in the flesh teaches believers how to embrace their weaknesses, rely on God's grace, and find strength in the midst of suffering.

Understanding the paradox of strength in weakness transforms how we view our struggles. Instead of seeing them as obstacles, we can see them as opportunities for God's power to be displayed in our lives. This perspective fosters humility, deepens our reliance on God, and strengthens our faith.

Paul's example encourages believers to trust in the sufficiency of God's grace and to find peace and strength in His presence. By embracing our weaknesses and relying on God's grace, we can experience the transformative power of suffering and bear witness to God's incredible love and strength.

In this way, Paul's teaching becomes a practical and powerful guide for Christian living, helping believers navigate their struggles with faith and confidence in God's unending grace. Through our weaknesses, God's strength is made perfect, and His love is revealed in profound and transformative ways.

Love in the Midst of Suffering: How Love Sustains and Empowers During Trials

Suffering is an inevitable part of the human experience, and how we navigate these trials can significantly impact our spiritual growth and overall well-being. In the midst of suffering, love—both divine and human—plays a crucial role in sustaining and empowering us. This chapter explores how love sustains and empowers believers during trials, drawing insights from biblical teachings and practical examples.

The Sustaining Power of God's Love

God's love is a constant and unwavering source of strength for believers, especially during times of suffering. Understanding and experiencing God's love can profoundly impact how we endure and overcome trials.

God's Presence in Suffering

1. Assurance of God's Presence:

- Psalm 23:4: "Even though I walk through the darkest valley, I will fear no evil, for you are with me; your rod and your staff, they comfort me."

- The assurance of God's presence brings comfort and peace in the midst of suffering. Knowing that God is with us, guiding and protecting us, helps alleviate fear and anxiety.

2. God's Faithfulness:

- Lamentations 3:22-23: "Because of the Lord's great love we are not consumed, for his compassions never fail. They are new every morning; great is your faithfulness."

- God's faithfulness ensures that His love and compassion are always available to us. His unwavering commitment to us provides a stable foundation during unstable times.

The Comfort of God's Love

1. God's Comfort:

- 2 Corinthians 1:3-4: "Praise be to the God and Father of our Lord Jesus Christ, the Father of compassion and the God of all comfort, who comforts us in all our troubles."

- God's love provides comfort in all our troubles. His presence, promises, and peace soothe our hearts and minds, helping us to endure suffering with hope.

2. Strength in Weakness:

- 2 Corinthians 12:9: "But he said to me, 'My grace is sufficient for you, for my power is made perfect in weakness.'"

- God's grace, a manifestation of His love, is sufficient for us. In our weakness, His power is made perfect, giving us the strength to persevere through trials.

The Hope of God's Love

1. Future Glory:

- Romans 8:18: "I consider that our present sufferings are not worth comparing with the glory that will be revealed in us."

- God's love assures us of future glory that far outweighs our present sufferings. This hope sustains us, knowing that our trials are temporary and that eternal joy awaits us.

2. Unshakeable Love:

- Romans 8:38-39: "For I am convinced that neither death nor life, neither angels nor demons, neither the present nor the future, nor any powers, neither height nor depth, nor anything else in all creation, will be able to separate us from the love of God that is in Christ Jesus our Lord."

- Nothing can separate us from God's love. This unshakeable assurance empowers us to face suffering with confidence, knowing that God's love will never fail.

The Empowering Role of Human Love

In addition to God's love, the love and support of others play a significant role in sustaining and empowering us during trials. Human love, expressed through compassion, encouragement, and practical help, can make a profound difference in how we endure suffering.

The Support of Community

1. Bearing Each Other's Burdens:

- Galatians 6:2: "Carry each other's burdens, and in this way you will fulfill the law of Christ."

- The love of a supportive community helps to bear the weight of our burdens. Sharing our struggles with others and receiving their support can lighten the load and provide much-needed encouragement.

2. Encouragement and Comfort:

- 1 Thessalonians 5:11: "Therefore encourage one another and build each other up, just as in fact you are doing."

- Encouraging words and actions from fellow believers can uplift our spirits and strengthen our resolve to endure. Comforting each other in times of distress fosters a sense of solidarity and hope.

Acts of Compassion

1. Practical Help:

- James 2:15-16: "Suppose a brother or a sister is without clothes and daily food. If one of you says to them, 'Go in peace; keep warm and well fed,' but does nothing about their physical needs, what good is it?"

- Acts of compassion, such as providing food, clothing, or financial assistance, demonstrate love in tangible ways. Practical help meets immediate needs and shows that we are not alone in our struggles.

2. Presence and Empathy:

- Romans 12:15: "Rejoice with those who rejoice; mourn with those who mourn."

- Simply being present with someone in their suffering, listening to them, and empathizing with their pain can be incredibly powerful. This shared experience of love and empathy strengthens bonds and provides emotional support.

The Healing Power of Love

1. Emotional Healing:

- Proverbs 17:17: "A friend loves at all times, and a brother is born for a time of adversity."

- The consistent love and support of friends and family can bring emotional healing. Knowing that we are loved and supported provides comfort and reassurance during difficult times.

2. Spiritual Growth:

- Ephesians 4:15-16: "Instead, speaking the truth in love, we will grow to become in every respect the mature body of him who is the head, that is, Christ. From him the whole body, joined and held together by every supporting ligament, grows and builds itself up in love, as each part does its work."

- Love within the community of believers promotes spiritual growth and maturity. Through mutual support and encouragement, we grow stronger in our faith and more resilient in the face of trials.

Practical Examples of Love in the Midst of Suffering

Living out love in the midst of suffering involves both receiving and giving love. Here are practical examples of how love can sustain and empower us during trials.

Receiving Love

1. Accepting Help:

- Opening Up: Be willing to share your struggles with trusted friends and family members. Allow them to offer help and support, whether through practical assistance or emotional encouragement.

- Seeking Prayer: Reach out for prayer support from your church community. Knowing that others are interceding for you can provide great comfort and strength.

2. Finding Comfort in God's Love:

- Meditating on Scripture: Spend time reading and meditating on Bible verses that speak of God's love and faithfulness. Let His promises reassure and strengthen you.

- Prayer and Worship: Engage in regular prayer and worship, drawing near to God and experiencing His comforting presence.

Giving Love

1. Offering Support:

- Practical Assistance: Provide practical help to those in need, such as preparing meals, running errands, or offering financial support. Your acts of kindness can make a significant difference in their lives.

- Emotional Support: Be present with those who are suffering. Listen to them, offer words of encouragement, and empathize with their pain.

2. Fostering Community:

- Building Relationships: Cultivate strong, loving relationships within your church and community. A network of supportive relationships provides a foundation of love and care.

- Creating Safe Spaces: Create safe spaces where people can share their struggles without fear of judgment. Encourage openness and honesty, fostering an environment of mutual support and compassion.

Conclusion

Love plays a crucial role in sustaining and empowering believers during times of suffering. God's love provides the ultimate source of comfort, strength, and hope, assuring us of His presence and faithfulness. In addition to divine love, human love expressed through the support of community, acts of compassion, and the healing power of empathy can significantly impact how we navigate trials.

By embracing and embodying love in the midst of suffering, believers can find the strength to endure and the hope to persevere. Love sustains us, empowers us, and transforms our suffering into opportunities for growth and deeper reliance on God.

Through both receiving and giving love, we reflect the heart of Christ and demonstrate the transformative power of the gospel. In this way, love becomes a practical and powerful guide for Christian living, helping us navigate the challenges of life with faith, hope, and unwavering confidence in God's unfailing love.

The Paradox of Power in Weakness: God's Strength Made Perfect in Human Weakness

The Christian life is often marked by paradoxes that challenge our understanding and expectations. One of the most profound paradoxes is the concept of strength in weakness, as articulated by Apostle Paul in 2 Corinthians 12:7-10. This passage reveals how God's strength is made perfect in human weakness, offering a transformative perspective on suffering and the role of divine power in our lives. This chapter explores the paradox of power in weakness, emphasizing how love sustains and empowers us during trials.

Paul's Experience with Weakness

Paul's personal testimony in 2 Corinthians 12:7-10 provides a powerful illustration of how God's strength is manifested in human weakness. His experience with the "thorn in the flesh" offers valuable insights into the nature of divine power and human vulnerability.

The Thorn in the Flesh

1. Persistent Affliction:

   - Verse 7: "Therefore, in order to keep me from becoming conceited, I was given a thorn in my flesh, a messenger of Satan, to torment me."

- Paul describes his thorn as a persistent and tormenting affliction, which served to keep him humble and reliant on God.

2. Humbling Experience:

- The thorn was a means to prevent pride and to ensure that Paul remained dependent on God's grace rather than his own abilities or spiritual experiences.

Paul's Plea and God's Response

1. Pleading for Relief:

- Verse 8: "Three times I pleaded with the Lord to take it away from me."

- Paul's repeated pleas for relief highlight his human vulnerability and desire for the affliction to be removed.

2. Divine Answer:

- Verse 9: "But he said to me, 'My grace is sufficient for you, for my power is made perfect in weakness.'"

- God's response redirected Paul's focus from seeking relief to embracing divine grace. The sufficiency of God's grace became the foundation for Paul's strength.

Embracing Weakness and Finding Strength

1. Boasting in Weakness:

- Verse 9: "Therefore I will boast all the more gladly about my weaknesses, so that Christ's power may rest on me."

- Paul learned to boast in his weaknesses because it was through them that Christ's power was most evident.

2. Finding Contentment:

- Verse 10: "That is why, for Christ's sake, I delight in weaknesses, in insults, in hardships, in persecutions, in difficulties. For when I am weak, then I am strong."

- Paul's perspective shifted to finding contentment and even delight in weaknesses, recognizing that they were opportunities for God's power to be revealed.

The Paradox of Power in Weakness

The concept of power in weakness is a fundamental aspect of the Christian faith. It challenges conventional wisdom and reveals profound truths about the nature of God's strength and our dependence on Him.

Understanding Divine Power

1. God's Sovereign Power:

- Creator and Sustainer: God's power is sovereign and supreme. He is the Creator and Sustainer of the universe, and His power is unmatched and limitless.

- Redemptive Power: God's power is also redemptive, working to restore and renew. It is through His power that salvation is accomplished and lives are transformed.

2. Manifested in Human Weakness:

- Paradoxical Nature: The paradox lies in the fact that God's power is most clearly seen and perfected in human weakness. This counterintuitive truth emphasizes that human frailty is the canvas for divine strength.

- Dependence on God: Human weakness necessitates dependence on God, allowing His power to work through us. This dependence glorifies God, as it becomes evident that the strength comes from Him and not from us.

Embracing Our Weaknesses

1. Acknowledging Limitations:

- Humility: Embracing weakness begins with humility—acknowledging our limitations and our need for God. It involves recognizing that we cannot navigate life's challenges on our own.

- Vulnerability: Being open about our weaknesses and vulnerabilities allows God's power to work in and through us. Vulnerability fosters genuine relationships and community support.

2. Finding Strength in God:

- Reliance on Grace: Relying on God's grace means trusting that His strength is sufficient for every challenge we face. His grace empowers us to endure and overcome.

- Continuous Dependence: Embracing weakness involves continuous, daily dependence on God. It is a posture of surrender and trust in His provision and power.

Practical Implications for Believers

Understanding the paradox of power in weakness has profound practical implications for how believers navigate suffering and challenges. It shapes our attitudes, actions, and relationships.

Living with Humility and Dependence

1. Daily Surrender:

- Prayer and Devotion: Cultivate a habit of daily surrender through prayer and devotion. Seek God's guidance and strength in every aspect of life.

- Acknowledging Need: Regularly acknowledge your need for God's help and rely on His strength rather than your own.

2. Embracing Vulnerability:

- Openness in Community: Be open about your struggles and weaknesses within your faith community. Vulnerability fosters deeper connections and mutual support.

- Seeking Support: Don't hesitate to seek support and encouragement from others. Allowing others to help you is an expression of humility and interdependence.

Finding Strength in God's Grace

1. Trusting God's Sufficiency:

- Resting in His Promises: Trust that God's grace is sufficient for every challenge. Rest in His promises and rely on His strength to sustain you.

- Contentment in Christ: Find contentment in Christ, knowing that His power is made perfect in your weakness. This contentment brings peace and confidence in the midst of trials.

2. Celebrating God's Power:

- Testifying to God's Strength: Share testimonies of how God's power has been evident in your weaknesses. Celebrate His strength and give Him glory for His work in your life.

- Encouraging Others: Encourage others by reminding them of God's sufficiency and strength. Help them see their weaknesses as opportunities for God's power to be revealed.

Serving Others in Love

1. Compassionate Ministry:

- Empathy in Action: Use your experiences of weakness and suffering to empathize with others and serve them compassionately. Your journey can provide comfort and hope to those facing similar challenges.

- Acts of Service: Engage in acts of service that demonstrate God's love and strength. Whether through practical help, emotional support, or spiritual encouragement, serve others with a heart of compassion.

2. Building Community:

- Fostering Unity: Foster unity within your faith community by embracing humility and vulnerability. Encourage an environment where everyone feels supported and valued.

- Strengthening Bonds: Strengthen the bonds of love and support within your community by being present, listening, and offering help to those in need.

Conclusion

The paradox of power in weakness is a profound and transformative truth that challenges our conventional understanding of strength and vulnerability. Paul's experience with his thorn in the flesh reveals how God's strength is made perfect in human weakness, offering a powerful perspective on suffering and divine power.

Understanding and embracing this paradox transforms how believers navigate trials and challenges. It calls us to live with humility, depend on God's grace, and find strength in His sufficiency. By acknowledging our weaknesses and relying on God's power, we experience His strength in profound and life-changing ways.

This paradox also has practical implications for how we live out our faith in the community. It encourages us to be vulnerable, seek support, and serve others with compassion. By doing so, we foster a loving and supportive community that reflects the heart of Christ and demonstrates the transformative power of the gospel.

In this way, the paradox of power in weakness becomes a practical and powerful guide for Christian living, helping us navigate the challenges of life with faith, hope, and unwavering confidence in God's unfailing love and strength. Through our weaknesses, God's power is revealed, and His love is made manifest in and through us.

CHAPTER 07

LOVE AND HOLINESS

1 Thessalonians 4:1-12: Living to Please God

In his letter to the Thessalonians, Apostle Paul provides practical instructions on how to live a life that pleases God, emphasizing the importance of sanctification and love. 1 Thessalonians 4:1-12 highlights the relationship between holiness and love, showing that a life dedicated to pleasing God is marked by both moral purity and genuine love for others. This chapter explores the connection between sanctification and love, drawing insights from Paul's teachings to understand how these two aspects of the Christian life are intertwined.

Living to Please God

Paul begins this section by urging the Thessalonians to live in a way that pleases God. This call to a holy life is not merely about avoiding sin but actively pursuing a life that reflects God's character and love.

The Call to Sanctification

1. Instructions from the Lord:

- Verse 1: "As for other matters, brothers and sisters, we instructed you how to live in order to please God, as in fact you are living. Now we ask you and urge you in the Lord Jesus to do this more and more."

- Paul reminds the Thessalonians of the instructions they received on how to live to please God and encourages them to continue growing in this way of life.

2. Sanctification as God's Will:

- Verse 3: "It is God's will that you should be sanctified: that you should avoid sexual immorality."

- Sanctification, or the process of becoming holy, is clearly stated as God's will for believers. This involves abstaining from behaviors that are contrary to God's standards, such as sexual immorality.

Holiness and Moral Purity

1. Control Over the Body:

- Verse 4: "That each of you should learn to control your own body in a way that is holy and honorable."

- Holiness involves exercising self-control and honoring God with our bodies. This includes avoiding impurity and living in a way that reflects God's holiness.

2. Distinction from the World:

- Verse 5: "Not in passionate lust like the pagans, who do not know God."

- Believers are called to live differently from those who do not know God. This distinction is marked by a commitment to purity and a rejection of behaviors driven by lust.

3. Respect for Others:

- Verse 6: "And that in this matter no one should wrong or take advantage of a brother or sister. The Lord will punish all those who commit such sins, as we told you and warned you before."

- Holiness also involves treating others with respect and integrity, avoiding any actions that would harm or exploit them.

The Relationship Between Holiness and Love

Paul's teachings in 1 Thessalonians 4:1-12 highlight that true holiness is inseparable from genuine love. Sanctification is not just about personal purity but also about how we love and treat others.

Love as the Fulfillment of Holiness

1. Increasing in Love:

- Verse 9: "Now about your love for one another we do not need to write to you, for you yourselves have been taught by God to love each other."

- Paul acknowledges the Thessalonians' love for one another, which they have been taught by God. This love is a key component of living a holy life.

2. Loving Others More and More:

- Verse 10: "And in fact, you do love all of God's family throughout Macedonia. Yet we urge you, brothers and sisters, to do so more and more."

- Just as believers are called to grow in sanctification, they are also called to grow in love. Loving others more and more is part of the continual process of becoming holy.

Practical Expressions of Love

1. Leading a Quiet Life:

- Verse 11: "And to make it your ambition to lead a quiet life: You should mind your own business and work with your hands, just as we told you."

- Love is expressed through living a peaceful and responsible life. This involves avoiding unnecessary conflicts, focusing on one's own responsibilities, and contributing positively to the community.

2. Earning the Respect of Outsiders:

- Verse 12: "So that your daily life may win the respect of outsiders and so that you will not be dependent on anybody."

- A life marked by love and holiness earns the respect of those outside the faith. It serves as a testimony to the transformative power of the gospel and the integrity of the believer.

Practical Implications for Believers

Understanding the relationship between holiness and love has profound practical implications for how believers live out their faith. It shapes our attitudes, behaviors, and interactions with others.

Pursuing Holiness

1. Personal Sanctification:

- Daily Commitment: Make a daily commitment to pursue holiness in every aspect of life. This includes seeking God's guidance through prayer and Scripture and making choices that reflect His standards.

- Accountability: Engage in accountability relationships with fellow believers who can provide support, encouragement, and correction in the pursuit of holiness.

2. Avoiding Temptations:

- Setting Boundaries: Establish clear boundaries to avoid situations that may lead to moral compromise. This includes being mindful of what you watch, read, and the company you keep.

- Seeking God's Help: Rely on the Holy Spirit for strength to overcome temptations and to cultivate self-control and purity.

Growing in Love

1. Loving One Another:

- Active Love: Demonstrate love through actions, not just words. Look for practical ways to serve and support others within the church and the broader community.

- Forgiveness and Grace: Practice forgiveness and extend grace to others, recognizing that love covers a multitude of sins (1 Peter 4:8).

2. Building Community:

- Fostering Relationships: Build strong, loving relationships within your church community. Engage in fellowship, small groups, and other activities that promote unity and mutual support.

- Encouraging Growth: Encourage others in their spiritual growth and in their pursuit of holiness. Offer support, prayer, and practical help as needed.

Living a Life of Integrity

1. Exemplary Conduct:

- Integrity in Actions: Strive to live a life of integrity, where your actions align with your professed beliefs. This includes being honest, reliable, and ethical in all dealings.

- Witness to the World: Recognize that your conduct serves as a witness to those outside the faith. Living a life of integrity and love can draw others to Christ.

2. Engaging with Society:

- Positive Contribution: Engage positively with society, contributing to the common good. This includes working diligently, respecting others, and being a source of peace and stability in your community.

- Advocacy and Justice: Advocate for justice and righteousness in your community, reflecting God's love and holiness in addressing social issues.

Conclusion

Paul's teaching in 1 Thessalonians 4:1-12 provides a comprehensive understanding of the relationship between holiness and love. True holiness is not merely about personal purity but also about how we love and treat others. Sanctification involves growing in love, leading a responsible and peaceful life, and earning the respect of those outside the faith.

Understanding and embracing this relationship transforms how believers live out their faith. It calls us to pursue personal sanctification, grow in love, and live lives of integrity and positive contribution to society. By doing so, we reflect God's character and demonstrate the transformative power of the gospel.

The pursuit of holiness and the practice of love are inseparable. As believers grow in holiness, their capacity to love increases, and as they grow in love, their lives more fully reflect the holiness of God. This dynamic relationship shapes individuals and communities according to God's perfect will, advancing His kingdom on earth.

In this way, Paul's teaching becomes a practical and powerful guide for Christian living, helping believers navigate the challenges of life with faith, hope, and unwavering confidence in God's unfailing love and holiness. Through our pursuit of sanctification and love, we become a testament to God's work in our lives and a beacon of His grace to the world.

Brotherly Love: Encouraging and Increasing in Love for One Another

In his letters, Apostle Paul frequently emphasizes the importance of brotherly love within the Christian community. 1 Thessalonians 4:9-10 specifically addresses this theme, urging believers to continue growing in their love for one another. Brotherly love is a reflection of God's love and is foundational to a healthy, vibrant church. This chapter explores the nature of brotherly love, how it can be encouraged and increased, and its significance for individual believers and the broader church community.

The Nature of Brotherly Love

Brotherly love, or "philadelphia" in Greek, refers to the affection and care believers are to have for one another, akin to the love between siblings. This type of love is marked by deep commitment, selflessness, and mutual support.

Characteristics of Brotherly Love

1. Affection and Care:

- Genuine Affection: Brotherly love involves genuine affection for one another, reflecting the familial bond among believers. This affection is not superficial but rooted in the shared identity in Christ.

- Mutual Care: It is characterized by a commitment to caring for each other's well-being, offering support in times of need, and rejoicing in times of blessing.

2. Selflessness and Sacrifice:

- Putting Others First: Brotherly love is selfless, prioritizing others' needs and interests above one's own. It involves making sacrifices to help and support fellow believers.

- Sacrificial Service: Just as Christ laid down His life for us, brotherly love calls for sacrificial service, whether through acts of kindness, financial help, or emotional support.

3. Unity and Harmony:

- Promoting Unity: Brotherly love fosters unity within the church, breaking down barriers and promoting a sense of belonging and togetherness.

- Resolving Conflicts: It encourages resolving conflicts with grace and forgiveness, maintaining harmony and peace within the community.

Encouraging Brotherly Love

Paul commends the Thessalonians for their love but urges them to increase it more and more. Encouraging and growing in brotherly love requires intentionality and practical steps that foster deeper relationships and a supportive community.

Fostering a Culture of Love

1. Teaching and Preaching:

- Biblical Instruction: Regular teaching and preaching on the importance of love, using Scriptures that emphasize God's love and the call to love one another, helps to cultivate a culture of love.

- Role Modeling: Leaders should model brotherly love in their interactions, providing a tangible example for others to follow.

2. Creating Opportunities for Fellowship:

- Small Groups: Establishing small groups or home fellowships where believers can build deeper relationships, share life experiences, and support each other.

- Church Activities: Organizing church activities and events that foster fellowship, such as meals, outings, and service projects.

Practicing Brotherly Love

1. Acts of Kindness:

- Helping Hands: Providing practical help to those in need, such as assisting with chores, offering rides, or providing meals during difficult times.

- Random Acts of Kindness: Engaging in random acts of kindness to brighten someone's day and show care, such as leaving encouraging notes or small gifts.

2. Emotional and Spiritual Support:

- Listening Ear: Being available to listen and offer emotional support to those who are struggling, providing a safe space for them to share their burdens.

- Prayer and Encouragement: Regularly praying for one another and offering words of encouragement and Scripture to uplift and strengthen fellow believers.

Building Strong Relationships

1. Intentional Connections:

- Reaching Out: Intentionally reaching out to new members or those who may feel isolated, making an effort to include them in the community.

- One-on-One Meetings: Scheduling one-on-one meetings or coffee dates to get to know others on a deeper level and build strong personal connections.

2. Conflict Resolution:

- Addressing Issues: Addressing conflicts directly and with love, seeking to understand and resolve differences in a way that promotes reconciliation and unity.

- Forgiveness and Grace: Practicing forgiveness and extending grace, recognizing that love covers a multitude of sins (1 Peter 4:8).

Increasing in Brotherly Love

Paul's exhortation to the Thessalonians to increase their love more and more indicates that there is always room for growth in our expressions of love. Increasing in brotherly love involves deepening our commitment to one another and continually seeking ways to love more effectively.

Personal Commitment to Growth

1. Self-Reflection:

- Assessing Love: Regularly assessing our own expressions of love and identifying areas where we can grow. This involves being honest about our shortcomings and seeking God's help to improve.

- Setting Goals: Setting specific, achievable goals for increasing our love for others, such as reaching out to someone new each week or volunteering for a service project.

2. Spiritual Disciplines:

- Prayer and Devotion: Deepening our relationship with God through prayer and devotion, asking Him to fill our hearts with His love and to help us love others more fully.

- Studying Scripture: Studying Scriptures that emphasize love and applying their teachings to our daily lives.

Community-Wide Efforts

1. Encouraging One Another:

- Mutual Encouragement: Encouraging one another to grow in love through regular reminders, testimonies, and celebrations of acts of love within the community.

- Shared Vision: Cultivating a shared vision of a loving community, where everyone is committed to supporting and caring for each other.

2. Organized Initiatives:

- Service Projects: Organizing service projects that provide opportunities for members to serve together, strengthening bonds and demonstrating love in action.

- Mentorship Programs: Establishing mentorship programs where older or more experienced believers can guide and support younger or newer members in their faith journey.

Embracing Diversity and Inclusion

1. Valuing Differences:

- Celebrating Diversity: Embracing and celebrating the diversity within the church, recognizing that different backgrounds, perspectives, and gifts enrich the community.

- Inclusive Practices: Ensuring that church practices and events are inclusive and welcoming to everyone, regardless of their background or status.

2. Building Bridges:

- Cross-Cultural Relationships: Encouraging cross-cultural relationships and understanding, fostering a sense of unity and love that transcends cultural and social boundaries.

- Addressing Biases: Being proactive in addressing any biases or prejudices that may exist within the community, promoting equality and mutual respect.

Conclusion

Paul's teaching in 1 Thessalonians 4:9-10 emphasizes the importance of brotherly love within the Christian community. Brotherly love is characterized by genuine affection, selflessness, and a commitment to unity and harmony. Encouraging and increasing in this love involves intentional efforts to build strong relationships, provide support, and create a culture of love and inclusion.

As believers commit to growing in love for one another, they reflect the heart of Christ and strengthen the body of Christ. Brotherly love not only enhances the well-being of individual believers but also serves as a powerful testimony to the world of the transformative power of the gospel.

By continually seeking to love more effectively and to increase in love, believers contribute to a vibrant, healthy, and loving community that honors God and fulfills His purposes. In this way, Paul's exhortation becomes a practical and powerful guide for Christian living, helping believers navigate the challenges of life with faith, hope, and unwavering confidence in God's unfailing love.

Through the practice of brotherly love, the church becomes a beacon of light and hope, demonstrating the reality of God's love and drawing others into the fellowship of believers. This commitment to love transforms individuals and communities, advancing God's kingdom on earth and bringing glory to His name.

Living a Quiet Life: The Practical Outworking of Love in Everyday Conduct

In 1 Thessalonians 4:11-12, Apostle Paul provides practical advice for living a life that pleases God and exemplifies Christian love. He urges believers to aspire to live quietly, mind their own affairs, and work with their hands. This call to a quiet life reflects the practical outworking of love in everyday conduct. This chapter explores the concept of living a quiet life, how it manifests in daily actions, and its significance for the believer and the broader community.

The Call to Live a Quiet Life

Paul's exhortation to live a quiet life is grounded in the principles of love, humility, and responsibility. It is a call to lead a life that is peaceful, respectful, and diligent, demonstrating love through practical actions.

Understanding the Quiet Life

1. Aspiring to Quietness:

- Verse 11: "And to make it your ambition to lead a quiet life: You should mind your own business and work with your hands, just as we told you."

- Paul encourages believers to aspire to a quiet life, which involves a deliberate effort to cultivate peace, avoid unnecessary conflict, and focus on one's responsibilities.

2. Minding One's Own Affairs:

- Respecting Boundaries: Living a quiet life means respecting others' boundaries and not meddling in their affairs. It involves focusing on our own responsibilities and avoiding gossip or interference.

- Personal Responsibility: It also emphasizes the importance of taking care of our own duties and obligations, ensuring that we contribute positively to our community.

3. Working with Your Hands:

- Diligence and Industry: Paul advocates for hard work and diligence, highlighting the value of honest labor. Working with our hands not only provides for our needs but also allows us to contribute to the well-being of others.

The Relationship Between Love and Quiet Living

1. Love Through Peaceful Conduct:

- Promoting Harmony: A quiet life promotes harmony and peace within the community. By avoiding unnecessary conflicts and focusing on peaceful interactions, we demonstrate love and respect for others.

- Reducing Tensions: Peaceful conduct helps to reduce tensions and fosters a supportive environment where love can flourish.

2. Love Through Respecting Boundaries:

- Honoring Privacy: Respecting others' privacy and boundaries is a practical expression of love. It shows that we value their autonomy and personal space.

- Encouraging Independence: Encouraging others to manage their own affairs and responsibilities promotes independence and self-reliance, which are acts of love.

3. Love Through Diligent Work:

- Providing for Needs: Working diligently ensures that we can provide for our own needs and avoid becoming a burden to others. This self-sufficiency allows us to help those in need.

- Serving Others: Honest labor enables us to serve others effectively, whether through our professional roles or through acts of charity and service.

Practical Outworking of Love in Everyday Conduct

Living a quiet life involves specific actions and attitudes that reflect the practical outworking of love in our daily lives. These actions demonstrate our commitment to loving God and others through responsible and respectful living.

Cultivating Peaceful Relationships

1. Avoiding Conflict:

- Seeking Reconciliation: When conflicts arise, strive for peaceful resolutions. Approach disagreements with a spirit of reconciliation and forgiveness.

- Practicing Patience: Be patient with others, recognizing that everyone has different perspectives and challenges. Patience fosters understanding and reduces the likelihood of conflict.

2. Communicating with Kindness:

- Speaking Gently: Use gentle and kind words in your interactions. Avoid harsh or hurtful language, which can escalate conflicts and damage relationships.

- Listening Actively: Practice active listening, showing genuine interest in others' thoughts and feelings. This demonstrates respect and helps build strong, loving relationships.

Respecting Boundaries and Responsibilities

1. Mind Your Own Business:

- Avoid Gossip: Refrain from gossiping or spreading rumors. Gossip harms relationships and creates distrust within the community.

- Focus on Personal Growth: Concentrate on your own personal and spiritual growth. By improving ourselves, we set a positive example for others and contribute to a healthier community.

2. Take Responsibility:

- Fulfill Obligations: Be diligent in fulfilling your responsibilities, whether at work, home or within the church. Responsible behavior builds trust and reliability.

- Help When Needed: While respecting others' boundaries, be willing to offer help and support when it is needed. Balancing respect for independence with a readiness to assist demonstrates love and care.

Working with Diligence and Integrity

1. Honest Labor:

- Work Diligently: Approach your work with diligence and dedication. Honest labor not only provides for your needs but also allows you to contribute to the community.

- Maintain Integrity: Uphold integrity in all your work. Be honest, reliable, and ethical in your professional and personal endeavors.

2. Serving Others Through Work:

- Use Your Skills: Use your skills and talents to serve others. Whether through your profession or volunteer work, your efforts can make a significant positive impact.

- Charitable Giving: If you are financially able, use your resources to support charitable causes and help those in need. Generosity is a powerful expression of love.

The Significance of Living a Quiet Life

Living a quiet life has significant benefits for individual believers and the broader community. It enhances personal well-being, strengthens relationships, and serves as a powerful witness to the transformative power of the gospel.

Personal Well-Being

1. Inner Peace:

- Reduced Stress: A quiet life reduces stress and anxiety by avoiding unnecessary conflicts and focusing on peaceful living. Inner peace contributes to overall well-being and mental health.

- Contentment: Focusing on personal responsibilities and maintaining a peaceful demeanor fosters contentment. Contentment in turn enhances joy and satisfaction in life.

2. Spiritual Growth:

- Closer Walk with God: A quiet and disciplined life allows for deeper spiritual growth and a closer walk with God. It provides space for prayer, reflection, and communion with the Lord.

- Strengthened Faith: By relying on God's guidance and strength to live a quiet life, our faith is strengthened, and we grow more resilient in the face of challenges.

Strengthening Relationships

1. Building Trust:

- Reliability: By fulfilling our responsibilities and respecting others' boundaries, we build trust within our relationships. Trust is the foundation of strong, healthy connections.

- Consistency: Consistently living a quiet and respectful life demonstrates reliability and integrity, which strengthens bonds with family, friends, and community members.

2. Fostering Community:

- Supportive Environment: A community where individuals live quietly and respectfully fosters a supportive and loving environment. Such a community is marked by mutual respect, care, and encouragement.

- Unified Purpose: By focusing on peaceful living and diligent work, the community can work together toward common goals, promoting unity and cooperation.

Witness to the World

1. Exemplary Conduct:

- Reflecting Christ: Living a quiet life reflects the character of Christ and serves as a powerful testimony to others. It demonstrates the transformative power of the gospel in practical ways.

- Positive Influence: Our conduct can positively influence others, drawing them to the faith and encouraging them to explore the teachings of Christ.

2. Earning Respect:

- Verse 12: "So that your daily life may win the respect of outsiders and so that you will not be dependent on anybody."

- Living a quiet and responsible life earns the respect of those outside the faith. It shows that Christians are trustworthy, diligent, and loving, which can open doors for sharing the gospel.

Conclusion

Paul's exhortation to live a quiet life in 1 Thessalonians 4:11-12 provides practical guidance for how believers can reflect the love of Christ in their everyday conduct. A quiet life, marked by peaceful relationships, respect for boundaries, and diligent work, is a powerful expression of love and holiness.

By aspiring to live quietly, minding our own affairs, and working with our hands, we demonstrate love for God and others in tangible ways. This way of life not only enhances our personal well-being and strengthens our relationships but also serves as a compelling witness to the world.

As believers commit to living a quiet life, they contribute to a harmonious and supportive community that honors God and fulfills His purposes. In this way, Paul's teaching becomes a practical and powerful guide for Christian living, helping believers navigate the challenges of life with faith, hope, and unwavering confidence in God's unfailing love.

Through the practice of living a quiet life, the church becomes a beacon of peace, integrity, and love, demonstrating the reality of God's transformative power and drawing others into the fellowship of believers. This commitment to love and holiness transforms individuals and communities, advancing God's kingdom on earth and bringing glory to His name.

CHAPTER 08

LOVE AND THE LAST DAYS

1 Timothy 1:5: The Goal of Commandment

In 1 Timothy 1:5, Apostle Paul provides a succinct yet profound statement about the purpose of his instructions to believers: "The goal of this command is love, which comes from a pure heart and a good conscience and a sincere faith." This verse encapsulates the essence of Paul's teachings and emphasizes that love is the ultimate goal of all Christian instruction. This chapter explores the significance of love as the end goal of Paul's commands, its implications for believers, and how it shapes our understanding and conduct, especially in the context of the last days.

Love as the End Goal

Paul's assertion that love is the goal of the commandment highlights the centrality of love in the

Christian faith. It is not merely an abstract ideal but the practical outcome of a life transformed by Christ.

The Source of Love

1. A Pure Heart:

- Inner Transformation: Love originates from a pure heart, one that has been transformed by the Holy Spirit. This purity involves a heart cleansed from sin and aligned with God's will.

- Holiness and Integrity: A pure heart reflects holiness and integrity, essential qualities for authentic love. This purity enables believers to love selflessly and genuinely.

2. A Good Conscience:

- Moral Integrity: A good conscience is the result of living according to God's moral standards. It involves a sense of moral clarity and the ability to discern right from wrong.

- Peace of Mind: Maintaining a good conscience brings peace of mind and confidence in one's actions. It allows believers to love others without guilt or hidden motives.

3. A Sincere Faith:

- Genuine Belief: Sincere faith is a genuine, unwavering trust in God. It is the foundation of a believer's relationship with God and others.

- Faith in Action: This faith is not just intellectual assent but is demonstrated through actions motivated by love. Sincere faith compels believers to live out their beliefs in practical ways.

The Purpose of Commandments

1. Guiding Believers to Love:

- Instruction in Righteousness: Paul's commandments and instructions serve to guide believers toward a life characterized by love. They provide practical guidance for living out the principles of the gospel.

- Cultivating Love: The commandments are designed to cultivate love among believers, promoting behaviors and attitudes that reflect God's love.

2. Building a Loving Community:

- Unity and Harmony: By emphasizing love as the end goal, Paul aims to build a community marked by unity and harmony. Love fosters mutual respect, support, and cooperation.

- Witness to the World: A community that embodies love serves as a powerful witness to the world, demonstrating the transformative power of the gospel.

Implications for Believers

Understanding that love is the end goal of Paul's instructions has profound implications for how believers live out their faith. It shapes our attitudes, actions, and relationships, especially as we navigate the challenges of the last days.

Prioritizing Love

1. Central Focus:

- Above All Else: Recognize that love is the central focus of Christian living. Prioritize love in all aspects of life, ensuring that it guides decisions, behaviors, and interactions.

- Motivation for Actions: Let love be the motivation behind all actions. Whether in ministry, work, or personal relationships, act out of genuine love and concern for others.

2. Reflecting God's Character:

- Imitating Christ: Strive to reflect God's character by loving others as Christ loves us. This involves sacrificial love, humility, and compassion.

- Bearing the Fruit of the Spirit: Cultivate the fruit of the Spirit, which includes love, joy, peace, patience, kindness, goodness, faithfulness, gentleness, and self-control (Galatians 5:22-23).

Cultivating a Pure Heart, Good Conscience, and Sincere Faith

1. Heart Purity:

- Spiritual Disciplines: Engage in spiritual disciplines such as prayer, Bible study, and meditation to maintain a pure heart. Regularly confess sins and seek God's cleansing.

- Guarding the Heart: Protect the heart from influences that can corrupt it. Be mindful of what you consume, whether media, relationships, or activities.

2. Maintaining a Good Conscience:

- Ethical Living: Live ethically and uphold moral integrity in all areas of life. Make decisions that align with God's standards and maintain a clear conscience.

- Seeking Forgiveness: When mistakes are made, seek forgiveness and make amends. A good conscience is restored through repentance and reconciliation.

3. Strengthening Faith:

- Faith Practices: Strengthen faith through regular worship, fellowship, and service. These practices reinforce trust in God and commitment to His ways.

- Faith in Trials: Rely on faith during trials and challenges. Let sincere faith be the anchor that sustains and guides you through difficult times.

Living Out Love in the Last Days

In the context of the last days, the call to live out love becomes even more critical. Believers are to be vigilant, discerning, and steadfast, ensuring that love remains at the forefront of their lives.

Vigilance and Discernment

1. Guarding Against Deception:

- Spiritual Discernment: Be vigilant against false teachings and deception. Use discernment to recognize and reject anything that contradicts God's truth.

- Staying Grounded: Stay grounded in Scripture and the core tenets of the faith. Let God's Word be the standard by which all teachings and practices are measured.

2. Loving in Truth:

- Truth and Love: Ensure that love is always coupled with truth. Speak the truth in love, correcting and guiding others with gentleness and compassion (Ephesians 4:15).

- Authentic Love: Avoid superficial or hypocritical expressions of love. Strive for authenticity, allowing love to flow genuinely from a pure heart and sincere faith.

Steadfastness in Love

1. Enduring Love:

- Perseverance: Persevere in love, even in the face of persecution, hardship, or opposition. Let love be the steadfast anchor that holds firm during trials.

- Long-Suffering: Be patient and long-suffering, reflecting God's enduring love. Extend grace and forgiveness, even when it is challenging.

2. Active Love:

- Service and Sacrifice: Engage in acts of service and sacrifice, demonstrating love through tangible actions. Be proactive in seeking opportunities to help and support others.

- Community Engagement: Be actively involved in your community, both within and outside the church. Let your love be a beacon that draws others to Christ.

Conclusion

Paul's declaration in 1 Timothy 1:5 that the goal of the commandment is love encapsulates the essence of Christian living. Love, which arises from a pure heart, a good conscience, and a sincere faith, is the ultimate aim of all instruction and the foundation of a vibrant, faithful community.

Understanding that love is the end goal has profound implications for how believers navigate their faith, especially in the context of the last days. It calls for a prioritization of love, a commitment to maintaining purity, integrity, and genuine faith, and a vigilant, steadfast approach to living out love in a challenging world.

By embracing love as the central focus of their lives, believers reflect the character of Christ and demonstrate the transformative power of the gospel. This commitment to love not only strengthens individual faith but also builds a unified, supportive community that serves as a powerful witness to the world.

Through love, believers can navigate the complexities and challenges of the last days with faith, hope, and unwavering confidence in God's unfailing promises. In this way, Paul's teaching becomes a practical and powerful guide for Christian living, helping believers to embody the love of Christ and advance God's kingdom on earth.

Faith and a Good Conscience: The Interplay Between Love, Faith, and Moral Integrity

In 1 Timothy 1:5, Apostle Paul highlights the critical relationship between love, faith, and a good conscience. He asserts that the goal of his instruction is love, which flows from a pure heart, a good conscience, and sincere faith. This triad forms the foundation of Christian living, demonstrating how these elements interplay to produce a life that pleases God and effectively witnesses to others. This chapter explores the dynamic relationship between love, faith, and moral integrity, emphasizing their interdependence and their importance in the believer's life.

The Foundation of Love, Faith, and Moral Integrity

Paul's teaching in 1 Timothy 1:5 emphasizes that true Christian love arises from a heart transformed by faith and maintained by moral integrity. Understanding the foundation of each element provides insight into their interconnectedness.

Sincere Faith

1. Faith as the Basis of Relationship with God:

- Trust in God: Sincere faith is a genuine trust in God and His promises. It forms the basis of a believer's relationship with God, grounding them in His truth and guiding their actions.

- Living Faith: Faith is not merely intellectual assent but is demonstrated through actions. James 2:17 states, "Faith by itself, if it is not accompanied by action, is dead." True faith produces works that reflect God's love and character.

2. Faith and Love:

- Faith Expressed Through Love: Galatians 5:6 emphasizes that "the only thing that counts is faith expressing itself through love." Genuine faith manifests in loving actions, showing that faith and love are intrinsically linked.

- Love as Evidence of Faith: Love serves as the evidence of sincere faith. Jesus taught that love for one another would be the identifying mark of His disciples (John 13:35).

A Good Conscience

1. Moral Integrity:

- Clear Conscience: A good conscience involves living with moral integrity, maintaining a clear conscience before God and others. It reflects a life committed to God's standards of right and wrong.

- Peace of Mind: A good conscience brings peace of mind, knowing that one's actions align with God's will. This inner peace is essential for a stable and fruitful Christian life.

2. Conscience and Love:

- Guiding Behavior: A good conscience guides behavior, ensuring that actions are consistent with Christian values. This moral integrity fosters genuine love, free from hypocrisy or hidden motives.

- Enabling Love: A clear conscience enables believers to love others sincerely, without the burden of guilt or unresolved sin. It allows for honest, transparent relationships.

Pure Heart

1. Heart Transformation:

- Inner Purity: A pure heart is one that has been transformed by the Holy Spirit, cleansed from sin, and aligned with God's desires. It is the wellspring from which true love flows.

- Holiness: Purity of heart reflects holiness, a commitment to living according to God's standards. This purity is essential for authentic love, as it removes selfishness and deceit.

2. Heart and Love:

- Source of Love: Love originates from a pure heart, where God's love is deeply rooted. Matthew 5:8 states, "Blessed are the pure in heart, for they will see God." A pure heart enables believers to perceive and reflect God's love.

- Sustaining Love: A pure heart sustains love by continually seeking God's presence and guidance. It fosters a consistent and enduring love for others.

The Interplay Between Love, Faith, and Moral Integrity

The interplay between love, faith, and moral integrity creates a holistic and balanced Christian life. Each element supports and enhances the others, leading to a life that glorifies God and blesses others.

Love Flowing from Faith and Integrity

1. Faith as the Foundation:

- Rooted in Faith: Love is rooted in sincere faith, which provides the motivation and strength to love others. Faith in God's love for us compels us to love others in return.

- Faith Sustains Love: During challenging times, faith sustains love by reminding believers of God's unchanging love and promises. This faith encourages perseverance in loving actions.

2. Integrity Enhances Love:

- Guided by Conscience: A good conscience guides believers in loving others with purity and sincerity. Moral integrity ensures that love is not tainted by selfish motives or deceit.

- Transparent Love: Love that flows from a clear conscience is transparent and trustworthy. It fosters deep, meaningful relationships based on mutual respect and honesty.

Faith Strengthened by Love and Integrity

1. Love Reinforces Faith:

- Active Faith: Love puts faith into action, demonstrating its reality and power. Acts of love reinforce and strengthen faith, showing that it is alive and active.

- Encouraging Faith: Loving relationships within the Christian community provides encouragement and support, helping believers to grow in their faith.

2. Integrity Upholds Faith:

- Consistent Witness: Moral integrity upholds the witness of faith, showing that it is genuine and transformative. A good conscience validates the claims of faith by demonstrating its impact on one's life.

- Strengthening Trust: Living with integrity builds trust within the community and with those outside the faith. It shows that believers can be trusted because their actions align with their professed beliefs.

Integrity Supported by Faith and Love

1. Faith Encourages Integrity:

- Accountability to God: Faith in God provides accountability, encouraging believers to live with integrity. Knowing that they are accountable to God motivates them to maintain a good conscience.

- Empowerment by the Spirit: Faith in the Holy Spirit's empowering presence enables believers to live with integrity, overcoming temptations and challenges.

2. Love Promotes Integrity:

- Motivation to Live Rightly: Love for God and others motivates believers to live with moral integrity. It compels them to act in ways that honor God and benefit others.

- Integrity in Relationships: Love fosters integrity in relationships, ensuring that interactions are marked by honesty, respect, and trust.

Practical Applications for Believers

Understanding the interplay between love, faith, and moral integrity has practical implications for daily Christian living. It guides how believers interact with God, others, and the world around them.

Cultivating Sincere Faith

1. Deepening Relationship with God:

- Prayer and Devotion: Engage in regular prayer and devotion to deepen your relationship with God. Seek His guidance and strength to live out your faith authentically.

- Scripture Study: Study Scripture to understand God's promises and commands. Let His Word shape your beliefs and actions.

2. Faith in Action:

- Serving Others: Put your faith into action by serving others. Look for opportunities to demonstrate God's love through practical acts of kindness and service.

- Sharing Your Faith: Share your faith with others, using your words and actions to testify to God's goodness and love.

Maintaining a Good Conscience

1. Ethical Living:

- Upholding Standards: Uphold God's moral standards in all areas of life. Make decisions that align with His will and maintain a clear conscience.

- Seeking Forgiveness: When you fall short, seek forgiveness and make amends. A clear conscience is restored through repentance and reconciliation.

2. Transparency and Accountability:

- Honest Relationships: Be honest and transparent in your relationships. Build trust by being reliable and truthful in your interactions.

- Accountability Partners: Establish accountability relationships with fellow believers. Allow them to provide support and correction as you seek to live with integrity.

Demonstrating Pure Love

1. Selfless Actions:

- Putting Others First: Practice selfless love by putting others' needs and interests above your own. Look for ways to serve and support those around you.

- Sacrificial Giving: Be willing to make sacrifices to help others. Whether it's time, resources, or energy, sacrificial love reflects the heart of Christ.

2. Building Community:

- Fostering Unity: Foster unity within your church and community. Promote harmony and cooperation through acts of love and kindness.

- Encouraging Growth: Encourage others in their spiritual growth. Offer support, prayer, and practical help as they seek to deepen their faith and live with integrity.

Conclusion

Paul's teaching in 1 Timothy 1:5 underscores the vital relationship between love, faith, and moral integrity. These elements are interdependent, each enhancing and supporting the others to produce a life that glorifies God and effectively witnesses to others.

Understanding and embracing the interplay between love, faith, and a good conscience transforms how believers live out their faith. It calls for a deep, genuine trust in God, a commitment to moral integrity, and a love that flows from a pure heart. This holistic approach to Christian living fosters spiritual growth, strengthens relationships, and demonstrates the transformative power of the gospel.

By prioritizing love, cultivating sincere faith, and maintaining a good conscience, believers can navigate the complexities of life with confidence and grace. They become beacons of God's love, truth, and holiness, drawing others to Christ and advancing His kingdom on earth.

In this way, Paul's teaching becomes a practical and powerful guide for Christian living, helping believers embody the love of Christ and live out their faith with authenticity and integrity. Through this commitment to love, faith, and moral integrity, the church becomes a vibrant, unified community that reflects God's glory and serves as a testament to His transformative power.

Persevering in Love: Enduring in Love Amidst Apostasy and False Teachings

In the New Testament, Apostle Paul frequently addresses the challenges that believers face, particularly in times of apostasy and the spread of false teachings. In his letters, he emphasizes the importance of perseverance in love as a safeguard against these dangers. This chapter explores how believers can endure in love amidst the growing threats of apostasy and false teachings, drawing insights from Paul's writings and other New Testament teachings.

The Reality of Apostasy and False Teachings

Paul and other New Testament writers warned of the inevitability of apostasy and the proliferation of false teachings in the last days. Understanding these threats helps believers remain vigilant and steadfast in their faith.

Apostasy in the Last Days

1. Falling Away:

- 2 Thessalonians 2:3: "Don't let anyone deceive you in any way, for that day will not come until the rebellion occurs and the man of lawlessness is revealed, the man doomed to destruction."

- Apostasy, or falling away from the faith, is a significant concern in the last days. Paul warns that many will abandon their faith, leading to a widespread rebellion against God.

2. Signs of Apostasy:

- 1 Timothy 4:1: "The Spirit clearly says that in later times some will abandon the faith and follow deceiving spirits and things taught by demons."

- Signs of apostasy include abandoning the core tenets of the Christian faith, being led astray by deceiving spirits and embracing doctrines contrary to the gospel.

The Spread of False Teachings

1. False Teachers:

- 2 Peter 2:1: "But there were also false prophets among the people, just as there will be false teachers among you. They will secretly introduce destructive heresies, even denying the sovereign Lord who bought them—bringing swift destruction on themselves."

- False teachers will infiltrate the church, introducing destructive heresies and leading many astray. These teachings often deny fundamental truths about Christ and salvation.

2. Deception and Division:

- Romans 16:17: "I urge you, brothers and sisters, to watch out for those who cause divisions and put obstacles in your way that are contrary to the teaching you have learned. Keep away from them."

- False teachings cause division and confusion within the church. Believers are urged to be vigilant and to avoid those who promote doctrines contrary to the apostolic teaching.

The Call to Persevere in Love

In the face of apostasy and false teachings, believers are called to persevere in love. Love serves as both a defense against deception and a testimony to the enduring truth of the gospel.

Love as a Defense Against Deception

1. Grounded in Truth:

- Ephesians 4:15: "Instead, speaking the truth in love, we will grow to become in every respect the mature body of him who is the head, that is, Christ."

- Persevering in love involves being grounded in the truth. Speaking the truth in love helps believers grow in maturity and unity, safeguarding them against falsehoods.

2. Discernment:

- Philippians 1:9-10: "And this is my prayer: that your love may abound more and more in knowledge and depth of insight so that you may be able to discern what is best and may be pure and blameless for the day of Christ."

- Abounding in love, coupled with knowledge and discernment, enables believers to identify and reject false teachings. Love motivates the pursuit of truth and purity.

Love as a Testimony to the Gospel

1. Enduring Love:

- Matthew 24:12-13: "Because of the increase of wickedness, the love of most will grow cold, but the one who stands firm to the end will be saved."

- Jesus warned that in the last days, the love of many would grow cold due to increasing wickedness. However, those who persevere in love to the end will be saved, demonstrating the power of enduring love.

2. Love as a Witness:

- John 13:35: "By this, everyone will know that you are my disciples, if you love one another."

- Love is the distinguishing mark of Christ's disciples. In a world filled with deception and division, persevering in love serves as a powerful witness to the truth and transformative power of the gospel.

Practical Ways to Persevere in Love

Persevering in love requires intentionality and practical actions that strengthen faith, promote unity, and defend against deception.

Strengthening Faith

1. Deepening Relationship with God:

- Regular Prayer and Devotion: Maintain a regular practice of prayer and devotion to deepen your relationship with God. Seek His guidance and strength to persevere in love.

- Scripture Study: Immerse yourself in Scripture, allowing God's Word to shape your beliefs and actions. Study the Bible to understand and defend the truth of the gospel.

2. Faith in Community:

- Fellowship: Engage in fellowship with other believers to encourage and support one another in faith. Shared faith experiences strengthen resolve and build a sense of community.

- Accountability: Establish accountability relationships with trusted believers who can provide support, encouragement, and correction as needed.

Promoting Unity

1. Building Loving Relationships:

- Acts of Kindness: Demonstrate love through acts of kindness and service within your community. Look for practical ways to support and encourage others.

- Conflict Resolution: Address conflicts with a spirit of reconciliation and forgiveness. Promote harmony and unity within the church.

2. Encouraging Growth:

- Mentorship: Engage in mentorship relationships, either as a mentor or mentee. Encourage spiritual growth and maturity through shared experiences and mutual support.

- Teaching and Discipleship: Participate in teaching and discipleship programs that promote understanding of the faith and encourage living out the principles of the gospel.

Defending Against Deception

1. Vigilance and Discernment:

- Be Watchful: Stay vigilant against false teachings and deception. Be aware of the signs of apostasy and remain grounded in the truth.

- Discernment through Prayer: Pray for discernment to recognize and reject false teachings. Seek God's wisdom in understanding and applying His Word.

2. Speaking the Truth in Love:

- Correcting Gently: When encountering false teachings, correct them gently and with love. Approach others with a spirit of humility and a desire to guide them back to the truth.

- Promoting Sound Doctrine: Support and promote sound doctrine within your church and community. Encourage adherence to the core tenets of the Christian faith.

Conclusion

Persevering in love amidst apostasy and false teachings is a critical challenge for believers in the last days. Understanding the reality of these threats and the call to endure in love equips believers to navigate these challenges with faith and resilience.

Love, grounded in truth and coupled with discernment, serves as a powerful defense against deception and a testimony to the enduring truth of the gospel. By prioritizing love, strengthening faith, promoting unity, and defending against false teachings, believers can persevere in love and stand firm in their faith.

Paul's teachings, along with other New Testament exhortations, provide practical and powerful guidance for Christian living. Through intentional actions and a commitment to love, believers can reflect the character of Christ and demonstrate the transformative power of the gospel, even in the midst of apostasy and deception.

In this way, the call to persevere in love becomes a practical and powerful guide for Christian living, helping believers to embody the love of Christ, maintain their faith, and advance God's kingdom on earth. Through steadfast love and unwavering faith, the church can remain a beacon of hope and truth in a world increasingly marked by falsehood and division.

CONCLUSION

THE ENDURING LEGACY OF PAUL'S THEOLOGY OF LOVE

Conclusion: The Enduring Legacy of Paul's

Summarizing Paul's Teachings: Key Takeaways from Paul's Epistles on Love

Apostle Paul's teachings on love are woven throughout his epistles, offering profound insights and practical guidance for living a life that pleases God. Here are the key takeaways from Paul's theology of love:

1. Love as the Greatest Virtue:

- In 1 Corinthians 13, Paul elevates love above all other virtues, including faith and hope. Love is described as patient, kind, and selfless, enduring all things and never failing. It is the greatest of all virtues and the foundation of Christian living.

2. Love Fulfills the Law:

- Romans 13:8-10 teaches that love fulfills the law. By loving our neighbors as ourselves, we naturally fulfill the commandments. Love is the essence of God's law and the ultimate expression of His will for humanity.

3. Love and Christian Freedom:

- In Galatians 5:13-14, Paul connects love with Christian freedom. Believers are called to use their freedom to serve one another in love. This service, driven by love, is the true exercise of Christian liberty.

4. Love in the Body of Christ:

- Ephesians 4:1-16 emphasizes the role of love in maintaining unity and fostering growth within the church. Love binds the body of Christ together, enabling it to function harmoniously and mature spiritually.

5. Love and Sacrifice:

- Philippians 2:1-11 highlights the sacrificial nature of love, exemplified by Christ's humility and obedience to death on the cross. Believers are called to emulate Christ's sacrificial love in their relationships with others.

6. Love in the Midst of Suffering:

- 2 Corinthians 12:7-10 illustrates how love sustains and empowers believers during trials. God's strength is made perfect in weakness, and His love provides the grace needed to endure suffering.

7. Love and Holiness:

- 1 Thessalonians 4:1-12 connects love with holiness, showing that a life dedicated to pleasing God is marked by both moral purity and genuine love for others. Sanctification and love are intertwined, leading to a life that reflects God's character.

8. Persevering in Love:

- Amidst apostasy and false teachings, Paul calls believers to persevere in love. Love, grounded in truth and coupled with discernment, serves as a defense against deception and a testimony to the enduring truth of the gospel.

Application for Today: How Contemporary Christians Can Embody Paul's Theology of Love in a Modern Context

Paul's teachings on love are timeless and offer valuable guidance for contemporary Christians seeking to live out their faith in a modern context. Here are practical ways to embody Paul's theology of love today:

1. Prioritize Love in All Relationships:

- Make love the guiding principle in all interactions, whether with family, friends, colleagues, or strangers. Practice patience, kindness, and selflessness, striving to reflect Christ's love in every situation.

2. Engage in Acts of Service:

- Use your freedom in Christ to serve others. Look for opportunities to help those in need, both within the church and in the wider community. Service driven by love demonstrates the reality of the gospel.

3. Foster Unity in the Church:

- Promote unity and harmony within your church community. Encourage and support one another, using your gifts to build up the body of Christ. Address conflicts with grace and seek reconciliation.

4. Embrace Sacrificial Living:

- Follow Christ's example of sacrificial love. Be willing to make personal sacrifices for the benefit of others. This may involve giving your time, resources, or energy to support those in need.

5. Persevere in Love During Trials:

- In times of suffering or hardship, rely on God's love for strength and endurance. Maintain a loving attitude even when it's challenging, trusting in God's grace to sustain you.

6. Maintain Moral Integrity:

- Live with a pure heart, good conscience, and sincere faith. Uphold God's moral standards and let your actions be guided by love and integrity. This will serve as a powerful witness to those around you.

7. Guard Against Deception:

- Be vigilant against false teachings and apostasy. Ground yourself in the truth of God's Word and cultivate discernment. Speak the truth in love and correct falsehoods gently and respectfully.

A Call to Love: Encouraging Readers to Pursue a Life Characterized by the Love Exemplified in Christ and Taught by Paul

The teachings of Apostle Paul on love are not just theological concepts but practical guides for living a life that honors God and blesses others. As you reflect on Paul's theology of love, consider how you can integrate these principles into your daily life.

1. Commit to Love as Your Highest Goal:

- Make a conscious commitment to prioritize love in all aspects of your life. Let love be the driving force behind your actions, decisions, and interactions.

2. Reflect on Christ's Example:

- Continually reflect on the sacrificial love of Christ. Allow His example to inspire and challenge you to love others more deeply and selflessly.

3. Cultivate a Loving Heart:

- Spend time in prayer and meditation, asking God to fill your heart with His love. Seek to develop a heart that overflows with compassion, kindness, and grace.

4. Take Action:

- Put love into action through practical deeds of service and kindness. Look for ways to make a tangible difference in the lives of those around you.

5. Encourage Others:

- Encourage others to pursue a life of love. Share Paul's teachings on love with your community and inspire them to live out these principles in their own lives.

By embracing and living out Paul's theology of love, you can make a profound impact on the world around you. Love is the enduring legacy of Paul's teachings and the defining mark of a true disciple of Christ. As you pursue a life characterized by love, you will not only fulfill God's commandments but also reflect His glory and advance His kingdom on earth.

In the words of Paul, "And now these three remain: faith, hope, and love. But the greatest of these is love" (1

Corinthians 13:13). Let love be the hallmark of your life, shining brightly as a testament to the transformative power of the gospel.